HOW TO LOVE YOURSELF UNCONDITIONALLY

AF528983

SUMEDHA THAKUR
KIRAN THAKUR

An imprint of
Srishti Publishers & Distributors

Srishti Publishers & Distributors
A unit of AJR Publishing LLP
212A, Peacock Lane
Shahpur Jat, New Delhi – 110 049

editorial@srishtipublishers.com

First published by Launchpad,
an imprint of Srishti Publishers & Distributors in 2025

Copyright ©Sumedha Thakur and Kiran Thakur, 2025

10 9 8 7 6 5 4 3 2 1

This is a work of non-fiction, based on the authors' experiences and life-learnings. It provides practical solutions to everyday problems, but the recommendations given herein are in no way intended to be a substitute for professional advice and help.

The authors assert the moral right to be identified as the author of this work.

All rights reserved. No part of this publication may be reproduced, stored in a retrieval system, or transmitted, in any form or by any means, electronic, mechanical, photocopying, recording or otherwise, without the prior written permission of the Publishers.

Printed and bound in India

To my mother, guru, life coach, and teacher...

I am forever indebted to you for your unconditional love. Your strength and belief in me have shaped who I am today and will continue to guide me in the future. Because of the life lessons you imparted, I have learned to love myself unconditionally and always to be my authentic self. This book serves as a roadmap to your teachings that have influenced my life. Your lessons are a gift to the world, helping others find their way back to loving themselves for who they truly are. To infinity and beyond, thank you for always looking after me.

Contents

Chapter 1
Introduction

A Journey Back to Unconditional Self-Love

All humans are born with innate goodness and unconditional love within themselves, which they freely give to others. However, as we grow, the world around us begins to shape our minds and belief systems, often disconnecting us from our authentic selves. Depending on our environment, we may either evolve into our highest selves whilst retaining that innate goodness, or lose our way, trapped in emotional patterns rooted in childhood conditioning.

Many of us, in response to emotionally unsafe environments, develop survival mechanisms early in life. These often include unhealthy attachment patterns and self-abandonment, particularly when love from caregivers is conditional. We learn to hide our true selves to gain approval and affection, creating coping strategies that may help us survive childhood—but which eventually sabotage our adult lives.

We are living in a world revolving around vanity, greed, fame, power, and money—the stark opposite of our inner, rich world of human moral values that we experience emotionally. Before we explore the journey towards unconditional love and mastering emotional intelligence, let us examine what has caused humanity to create such a chaotic world in the first place. We need to understand the psychological barriers of the mind that have been causing us to suffer across centuries, and why we have always been living in survival mode as adults in this man-made world.

"Don't cry like a girl!" and, "Stop being so dramatic!" are two statements that have transcended borders, religions, and cultures, managing to reach every child across centuries. This has led to them not learning how to express themselves emotionally. As children, we learned not to love certain parts of ourselves because we never felt emotionally safe to express ourselves freely. This led to us becoming adults who are still, deep down, emotionally wounded children governed by the same fears that stopped us from accepting ourselves completely in our childhood.

Our emotional growth has been stunted, and the only way to nurture it is by developing a healthy, regulated nervous system through mastering our negative emotions and reprogramming our thoughts. We must move forward from survival mode and escape our self-created mental prison of psychological barriers based on societal belief systems and our perception of self and the world around us. Our ability to love and accept all parts of ourselves empowers us with the freedom to express our emotions and feel vulnerable. It provides us with the courage to start choosing ourselves first.

This slowly changes our perception of self as we build a healthy relationship with our inner child. As we make peace with our past, we let go of all the fears, resentment, and hurt that hold us back. Only then can we move forward by developing an emotionally healthy relationship with ourselves. Only our fears perceive emotional vulnerability as weakness, rather than the superpower it truly is. That is why how we see, treat, listen to, speak to, respect, and value ourselves directly reflects our thoughts about ourselves and the world around us. Until our minds are consumed by negative feelings and we feel trapped in survival mode, we will continue to feel miserable internally, and we will always seek external validation, by giving others power over us to make us feel emotionally safe as adults.

Our trauma stems from emotional wounds caused by lack of empathy, conditional love, abuse, neglect, and invalidation during our formative years. Often, caregivers themselves were wounded and passed down their emotional pain unconsciously. Realizing this helps us understand that many of our emotional responses are not truly ours—they are inherited patterns that we have the power to rewire.

Healing requires self-awareness, accountability, and the courage to feel our emotions. Those who choose healing take ownership of their pain and responsibility for their actions. They become survivors and creators of new narratives. In contrast, those who remain stuck in victimhood continue to project blame and stay emotionally trapped.

The journey to inner peace involves nurturing creativity, intuition, and a deep connection to one's core values. Emotional intelligence arises from understanding and accepting the full spectrum of human emotions. When we stop operating from survival mode and embrace emotional independence, we begin to live from a place of freedom and authenticity.

Imagine yourself as a house: your foundation built on empathy, love, trust, and compassion. With strong emotional scaffolding, this house becomes a sanctuary—not only for yourself but for others. It is stable, generous, and discerning, attracting only those who share its values. However, when societal constructs—rooted in fear, greed, comparison, and division—interfere, this house remains incomplete, dependent, and vulnerable.

The system is designed to promote emotional dependence. We are taught to measure our worth through money, success, appearances, and approval. From an early age, institutions strip us of creativity and emotional freedom, conditioning us to seek validation and survival through external means. We become cogs in a machine that keeps us disconnected from our true selves.

But love—real, unconditional love—has never been the problem. Love does not hurt. Attachment, dependency, fear of abandonment, and the inability to meet our emotional needs are what cause suffering. Most of what we call "love" today is simply emotional dependency, rooted in fear and unmet childhood needs.

Life has become a repetitive script: education, career, relationships, marriage, retirement. The storyline is dictated by money, fame, materialism, and societal expectations. However, if you step outside this script and observe, you will see that the only thing that makes you truly unique is your humanity. Your emotions, your compassion, your ability to love and grow—that is your essence.

The endless chase for material validation has hollowed us out. We seek to be liked more than we seek to be loved. We hoard for the future whilst ignoring the richness of the present. We repeat generational traumas within families, mistaking emotional dependence for love, never realizing that true freedom comes from emotional autonomy.

To break these patterns, we must stop abandoning ourselves. Your inner child is your guide. It whispers reminders to choose authenticity, to feel your feelings, and to create a new reality.

So begin here: love yourself, unconditionally. Listen to your inner voice. Feel your emotions. Choose your story. Be your own sanctuary.

Chapter 2

Set Yourself Free

How do you set yourself free in a world that tries to cage you even before you learn to speak correctly through the educational system? The key lies in accepting people for who they are instead of what you want them to be. Expectations come from a place where we put ourselves in their shoes and decide what actions would have been the right course of action, especially in times of need or want in our lives. However, understand that all you needed was yourself—that would make all the difference. All we need to become is our own best friend.

Our relationship with ourselves is one of the most important relationships we'll ever have, as we live in our heads 24/7. How we view ourselves becomes the most essential thing in the world. If we do not value ourselves, the world will never value us. This happens because we will accept mistreatment from others if we have not made an effort to value who we are in the first place. We will accept the love and care that we are familiar with and think we deserve because that is our understanding of love and care—it reflects how we treat ourselves.

That is why we live in survival mode, as this dogmatic societal world forces us to. We never get or give ourselves the chance to discover what love, care, compassion, or empathy truly is because we are too busy fighting with each other or the system to survive. We never think for ourselves or question the dystopian world that has been created, which sets us up for failure. Until we discover these wonderful human values and learn to give them to ourselves—to have first-hand experience of what true standards are—we will not be able to enter or discover thriving mode, which should be every human's basic living right in the first place.

Expecting someone who has never understood you to understand you all your life is foolish. There is a reason why you have never got along with certain people throughout your life. The best thing to do is minimize interactions and not engage much with such people. Always remember there is a reason why you have those emotional triggers, which such people seem to activate all the time—because they are the ones who installed them in the first place. Exposing ourselves constantly to those triggers by increasing interactions will not help us in the long run.

Anyone seeking perfection in various aspects of life—be it body, weight, looks, work, food, and so on—is living from ego and is in survival mode, where they are constantly judgmental and critical towards themselves. Such people share a negative relationship with themselves and have not yet discovered who they are; that is why their ego governs them, as they are driven by how others perceive them.

The dogmatic societal structure is based on people's emotional dependence on external factors and people to validate their existence.

Such people are the ones who consume entertainment, follow public figures for validation, and need constant distractions to feel important. Such people will be the most updated about who said what and what is happening worldwide, because that helps them regulate emotionally—they depend on others to regulate their emotions. They will be so out of touch with their own feelings because they have not had or given themselves any opportunity to discover who they are.

Understand that people can only meet you at the level they have met themselves. Anyone who does not know who they are and is emotionally unavailable to themselves will never understand you. It is not our job to blame them for not showing up for us; we need empathy for such people who do not even know how to show up for themselves in the first place. No one taught them, and they refused to learn. They are already living sad lives based on how others perceive them because their perception of themselves is negative, and they are constantly emotionally dependent on others to regulate their own emotions as adults.

What is worse than being a prisoner of your own mind and unable to escape it no matter what you do? Such people have to live with themselves, and that in itself is their punishment because they hate themselves and their existence. People who live in survival mode cannot stand solitude and will do anything to escape their own minds. People at war with themselves are not the ones you should seek whilst trying to find your peace. Their mental cage stops them from living and constantly makes them suffer by keeping them in survival mode; the last thing you need is their validation whilst searching for your solace.

Wish them well and move on from such connections that are nothing but sources of conflict when you are trying to find peace within.

They cannot give you what they do not have, and reaching out to them to validate your actions and feel at peace wastes your time, attention, and effort. Remember that your time is your currency here on earth—the time you have and are spending whilst living you will never get back, so be mindful and become the main character you should be in your own story. Be unapologetically yourself before the world tries to mould you as a follower or a survivor to suit the dogma of societal structure so that they can continue to rule over you by playing good cop versus bad cop in their self-created survival-of-the-fittest structure.

Sometimes, we gaslight ourselves by choosing people who are fulfilling one or two needs that we believe we cannot meet ourselves, or we trick ourselves into thinking that we need them to fulfil those needs by getting unhealthily attached to such people. Hence, we also neglect our emotional needs and become people-pleasers by making their emotional needs our own. We try to fulfil them so they can choose us by picking us. We do all this subconsciously; we are reminded of all our childhood memories of not being picked or not coming first based on marks, teachers' rejections, or our parents' disappointment based on academic performance.

So we try harder to be picked and liked this time without realizing that we are reliving childhood trauma and attaching our emotions to someone else. How they behave determines how we feel; the same trauma cycle of childhood gets repeated. We do not chase such people because we love them; we chase such people because we see them as a solution to our needs and as our saviour. Instead of becoming our own saviour by fulfilling our emotional needs independently, we try to please them for external validation—in the same manner we were focused on the external validation of teachers and parents to feel lovable as a child.

Understand that you are enough, and you were always enough; you do not need someone else to fulfil your needs just because the dogmatic societal structure is constructed in such a manner that we are made to feel that we need others to achieve the goals we have set for ourselves or to have our emotional needs fulfilled in life.

It is an individual journey; all you ever needed was yourself, and that belief in yourself to fulfil your emotional needs. Buddha, Jesus, or Mohammad did not achieve enlightenment in a group, so why are we living and doing everything as a group in the name of family structure created by dogmatic societal structure? Remember that your life has always been about you and no one else. Always put your emotional needs first, instead of neglecting your emotions because someone in your childhood made you feel you were not enough.

You are more than enough for yourself; you are here for yourself and no one else. So always put your emotional needs first by creating a safe haven, being authentic, and creating an emotionally healthy relationship with yourself as an adult. People with good hearts do not need to prove to others that they are good human beings through words; their actions will speak of their authenticity. Only a narcissist wants an audience because they believe they have a sense of grandiosity, and they need to be worshipped by the masses for the qualities and human values they embody. They always want to be liked by everyone and will not stand it when someone does not like them.

It is when we shine our light on the darkness that consumes us that we can see the beautiful colours of our shadow self, which is a part of us waiting for the light to shine upon it, just like light shows us the vivid colours of the sky, trees, and oceans. We all carry our beautiful colours within us, hidden in our shadows, just as the night is waiting to be discovered. We heal ourselves through self-love, trust, and acceptance. Our darkness is the most beautiful part of us, just like nature—always remember that. The parts that we consider ugly or unpleasant are the ones that need the most light and love from us. They need our unconditional love and acceptance the most.

Be and love your authentic self so fiercely that no one can make you feel wrong about your existence anymore. Imagine yourself as the pen that writes your story through the ink of life experiences; if you do not like how the story is shaping up, you have the power to change the narrative by changing the direction of your story.

Chapter 3

Developing Emotional Intelligence

How do we measure human emotional intelligence, you may ask? Our emotional growth regarding empathy is directly proportional to where we stand in terms of human intelligence. Here is the hierarchy of emotional intelligence that will show you how evolved humanity is in terms of human intelligence:

- Empathy for all living beings: they see everyone as one instead of seeing themselves as separate human beings.
- Empathy for selective living beings that are not a threat to human lives: consider the ones who are safe to humanity as their own.
- Empathy for living beings that they do not need to consume.
- Empathy for their community based on religion, nationality, caste, creed, purchasing power, and colour.

- ❖ Empathy for themselves and others only if they need them to fulfil their needs.
- ❖ Empathy only for themselves, living with hatred towards self and others: a victim mindset.
- ❖ Empathy only for themselves: they thrive on drama and show sadistic and vindictive behaviour to get back at the world and their immediate family, for the hurt they feel inside.
- ❖ Lack empathy for all living beings, but they have it for a very few selective humans.

Our conditional beliefs are why we are all stuck in survival mode, suffering and disconnected from our authentic selves. They create a fragment of man-made reality that does not exist as our internal reality when we attach who we are—in terms of our identities—to it, and the same is reflected in our external world. Such beliefs, just like storytelling, keep changing every 2,000 years, when a new civilization is born, and get rehashed as a brand-new script of life to be followed by the herds of the dogmatic societal structure, be it religious, cultural, national, or societal structure—every 200 years with a completely new generation.

If our mind cannot remember every word in a book, what makes us think that everything we tell ourselves is not a figment of our imagination but rather the truth? Our reality is what we create. The roadmap that brings us closer to our authenticity is aligning ourselves with our authentic truth based on human values of empathy, kindness, love, acceptance, compassion, care, trust, belongingness, and selflessness. Our accurate map to ending our sufferings is listening to our heart by always keeping it open and shunning the conditioning of the mind that puts our identities in box-based divisions that act as psychological barriers and prevent us from being human in the first place.

So we sell ourselves through stories to other human beings based on our perception of self; if it is negative, then all the stories we tell others will have a negative view of the world that surrounds us, so the people we talk about will be doing harmful things to us. At the same time, we will continue to play the victim without realizing that our perception of self, based on our unhealed emotional state, causes much suffering in the first place.

Then we try to control the narrative; how do we do that? By creating mouthpieces like our PR, through our family members, relatives, and friends, through gaslighting, brainwashing, and projecting a created version of reality as the truth. Like multi-level marketing, our narrative will be told to others, and then they will pass judgement like a court of law, either in our favour or choose not to get involved if they do not buy into the narrative being sold. This is how mob mentality is created, when everyone, instead of fighting their own battles, gives their precious time and attention to money hoarders, narcissists, entertainers, and so-called influencers, instead of giving it to themselves by reconnecting with their inner child and emotions.

When we do not value ourselves, we subconsciously give our attention in the form of our time to others instead of ourselves. Our attention is our power. The moment we hand over the key to our decision-making abilities to someone else by giving them control over us, due to our unresolved emotional wounds—resulting in insecurities—we will continue to keep ourselves in the loop of a follower's mentality.

Why do we crave attention, you may ask? We were never heard as children, and we had to slam doors, cry, and yell to convey our point. As adults, we do the same thing by constantly talking about ourselves because we want someone else to validate that our actions are correct. It is a set pattern from childhood to continually repeat what we feel to validate ourselves. So we continuously need that validation to feel good about ourselves or to increase our confidence.

However, in that process, we often abandon our intuition, which is our guide back to our authentic self, and make life decisions or choices based on the internal belief that we need this thing or these people to fulfil our emotional needs whilst living in survival mode. Our choices are not based on human values, where we see if we are feeling emotionally safe in someone's presence; we want to run away from our external environment (people) because we do not have the support of our internal environment or safety from within (healed emotional state).

So we do not choose our authenticity because, just like Rome, it cannot be built or found in a day, when we have been disconnected from our internal self (emotions) for ages. After all, we fell into the trap of a man-made belief system that perceives happiness as something based on everything external and built on vanity.

The vanity of the world is reflected in humans too; we are so fixated on our external appearance that we have forgotten to take care of our internal state, be it mental, emotional, or physical. We do not question what we put in our bodies, as long as it gets us external validation based on what we look like from the outside or how we are perceived by people. We fail to understand that people's perception of us reflects their own inner self (emotional state), so why are we giving someone else—who has not chosen to heal their emotional state and has remained toxic—power to dictate who we are?

Who we are is our internal character and conduct based on human values; that is our true self. Anything else is just noise and clutter.

When our loved ones pass away, whom do you remember or miss the most? The ones who loved you for who you were, right? Or do you miss the one who used to earn more money and treated everyone badly? So if we miss and love the people who provided us with an emotionally healthy and safe space to be our authentic selves, then why are we giving people with more bank balance or money hoarders power over us, all our lives, by idealizing them or revolving our lives around them to be like them?

Love is what we remember as a feeling. Even if people leave, they touch us in ways no one could because we feel heard, understood, and loved for our honest, authentic selves. It is and always has been an internal journey of finding yourself; it has nothing to do with external man-made things or societal constructs. It is your relationship with your self that is the cause of your sufferings; the more you develop emotionally, the more healing involves feeling whatever was bottled up. Instead of running away from your own company, sit with yourself and make a choice to fix where you think the disconnect is, that is causing you to run whenever you feel vulnerable.

Closing a tank full of unresolved feelings, neglecting it, and pretending it does not exist will not make the tank disappear. It will keep rusting; the water inside will start to smell, rust, and rot if we do not acknowledge its existence. That is what we have been doing to ourselves—focusing on our followers, likes, and what people say instead of opening our tank of emotions and seeing how many unhealed or unresolved issues we have.

We are all at different stages of our emotional journey; some have chosen not to heal their abandonment wounds and latch onto their family members as caregivers, by controlling their emotional state to feel safe, and some have decided to heal and break the generational trauma by going deeper to understand why they have these issues in the first place, which are causing them to suffer as humans.

In any family worldwide, one person would be obsessed with acquiring materialistic things of this dogmatic societal structure to win society's external validation; these are the ones who have fallen into the trap of the dogmatic societal structure and revolved their lives around it. Such people are always living in survival mode and are driven by their ego; they are deeply insecure and always need others to validate their feelings as they have never learnt how to regulate their own emotions independently. They continue the generational trauma of being emotionally unavailable by becoming narcissists, who hate themselves, with fragile egos and low self-esteem.

Our first emotional attachment is to the parent of the opposite sex, so if that parent is a narcissist, then the son or daughter will turn out to be a narcissist because, as a child, they got the message that he or she is unlovable. Such people stopped loving themselves due to this.

We hold resentment when we blame others for how they made us feel and choose not to voice or validate our emotions by acting and standing up for ourselves—by holding such people accountable for their actions as adults. No one else except you is responsible for how others make you feel. The actions anyone takes in their lives reflect how they feel internally; we have a full right to voice our feelings and set boundaries with people who have disrespected us in the first place. Expecting someone to act like us comes from a place of our inner reflection of our internal state.

Age has nothing to do with emotional intelligence; we all need to respect each other as humans, but wisdom does not grace the closed mind—the ones who love conditionally and are full of apathy towards others. Age is reflected in our bodies, but wisdom is reflected in our inner reality and self-perception, based on our emotional growth. Only the ones who do not let their circumstances define them but choose to lead their lives with an open heart and a curious mind will be the ones who are willing to embrace the unknown with open arms without any fear, because they understand that life is nothing but full of uncertainty.

Controlling life is like stopping a river and not being able to realize with time why it has become so lifeless in the first place. Going with the flow with an understanding that you are exactly where you need to be right now is the best way to understand the meaning of life. It comes with no guarantee and never has. Why waste your time feeling sorry when you have come here to experience all the human emotions and master them?

Our sufferings will continue no matter what until we choose to change our reality by understanding that it has always been an individual journey. Until we do not have a balanced emotional state from within, we will continue to suffer emotionally because we have not learnt how to regulate our emotional state healthily. Some people do not have a healthy relationship with themselves and can never stay alone. They will keep surrounding themselves with others to avoid their own company.

It is not our fault that we have never been taught to build a relationship with ourselves first; that inner voice you follow, listen to, and pay heed to is based on how you feel about yourself and the world. Imagine the shock one will get if one knows that one's inner voice reflects how one views oneself in one's own eyes. The only way people notice each other's mental health is when someone gets attacked or killed; it is only then that we are concerned or bothered about someone's mental state.

We fail to understand that anyone who has not been taught how to regulate and process their emotions will fail to understand how they are feeling or will struggle to voice their feelings, because they do not know how to express how they feel in the first place. The disconnect from our emotional state and how one feels is the leading cause of issues across the globe, and people, instead of sorting it out, fail even to understand the main reason for their emotional upheaval.

First, one should learn that no one else can be more important in your life's story than you. You are the main character of your story, and any decision you are taking or will take has to align with your innate desires or should make you feel emotionally safe on a human level. Anything that causes negative emotions or does not feel emotionally safe has to go. As shown in films, you were and always will be the main character of your life's story. It is all about you, and your decisions will continue to affect you in the long run.

The best way to function in today's society is to listen to what others have to say and contemplate it, but at the end of the day, go ahead with what your authentic self deems right. The more in line with our authentic self we are, the more true to our real self we will be. That is how one will continue to honour one's authentic self as one grows up. However, we need to be allowed to grow into our authentic selves as children.

Most of us attach our identities to man-made things, be it bank balances, brands, homes, cars, clothes, and so on, based on our likes and dislikes; we never give ourselves a chance to discover the depth of who we are in our authenticity as a person, which is based on human values of trust, loyalty, honour, respect, and so on. The human values we carry and embed in ourselves make us our true, authentic selves as adults—such as trustworthy, honourable, selfless, loyal, kind, giving, and so on. This makes us human; anything man-made or money-based represents our likes and dislikes; it has nothing to do with who we are as authentic human beings or our values.

Such external validation to feel good from the inside or to express individualism, if it is based on money or the purchasing power of brands, just shows that we have failed to evolve as human beings, wherein we did not even have an opportunity to discover what our human values are in the first place. All we have learnt to express our individuality is through purchasing wealth or brands and showing it off on social media or in society. Such people have the lowest human intelligence and have failed to evolve and grow emotionally. The child's emotional age gets stuck in them, and they never grow or develop and, at the same time, continue to pass the baton to their children as adults.

The evolution of the entire family, if influenced by the emotionally unevolved parent, would be the same as an undergrown child with volatile emotions, especially if the parent is of the opposite sex. Emotional growth is stunted in such families, and people can no longer move beyond people-pleasing tendencies. They are never taught to live for themselves; they are always taught about rules and regulations of society based on man-made things, be it religion, money, caste, creed, colour, purchasing power, and so on.

So why do we people-please? Even if we do not like someone, we tend to stay in touch or connected to such people in the name of relationships, friendships, relatives, or family. We tend to keep brushing whatever we feel under the carpet because we are taught to tolerate such people in the name of connections. We are never taught that we always have a choice to walk out if someone makes us feel emotionally unsafe, insecure, and threatened. We do not need their approval or validation to acknowledge our humanness or existence.

How can people who do not even know themselves validate your qualities or you when they have never discovered or met their genuine, authentic self? Such people will never validate your existence when they have not tried to find their own. Let it go, and let such people go. Imagine navigating your boat through the stillness of life, dropping the dead weight that pulls you down and does not allow you to move further in the vastness of life and the universe.

Accept people for who they are instead of what you want them to be. It gives us clarity and a reality check, providing us with the closure we never knew we needed to move on with our lives. Sometimes, seeing and accepting people for who they are is the closure we require. Stop seeing such people for what they want you to perceive based on the dogmatic societal image driven by ego and narcissism of a "good person or a human being."

Everyone who has played an essential role in your life, be it for good or bad, was there to teach you life lessons on what you need to be and what you need to avoid. The ones you loved unconditionally—

your caregivers—but were emotionally dependent on to validate your thoughts and actions, to have the feeling of emotional safety as a happy hormone booster, which you never got. The ones who gave you these emotional wounds taught you self-respect, trust, boundaries, and whatnot in this lifetime.

Our job is not to fight and blame them for the harm they caused us. Yes, giving your inner child justice is correct, but we must also accept people for who they are instead of questioning why they did what they did. We need to understand that they were available to us at the same level they were available to themselves; if they were emotionally unavailable to themselves, expecting them to validate the hurt and the pain that they have caused is fruitless as they will never understand the damage they have caused, as they are emotionally wounded themselves.

The only way to make peace with the past is to accept our caregivers for who they are instead of what we want them to be for us. We cannot determine if we can help change someone unwilling to change or take accountability for their actions. They played their part in teaching you not to be like them, to end your mind's sufferings. They were blaming you for the parts they did not like about themselves and projected their self-hatred onto you. It was never about who you were in the first place.

Our job is to acknowledge that whatever they say reflects the self they see in us and has nothing to do with our authentic selves. It was just a projection of the worst qualities they saw in themselves, and instead of accepting themselves for their good, bad, and ugly, for being human, their hatred for self was taken out on us as children. It was never our pain to bear or burden to carry.

They chose not to heal, but that does not mean we also have to continue the cycle of suffering that they decided not to break. With self-awareness and understanding that those beliefs were not who we are, we can choose to discover who we are no matter our age, to be the best version of our authentic selves. It might sound like a long journey, as it means shedding whatever you have been conditioned to believe that no longer serves you. Still, it is also a way out to a new life built on your terms, based on freedom of mind, and lived through authenticity in line with a contented and fulfilled heart.

Our hearts only understand the language of love, gratitude, and human values that make us feel alive as we live our authentic lives. Anything else is just the trick of the conditioned mind to save us by working in survival fight-and-flight mode that we can always choose to opt out of by refusing to be the hamster running directionlessly over a plan that is based on external milestones, which has nothing to do with emotional fulfilment internally.

We, as humans, always had and needed a purpose to be in line with our authentic selves; the shortcomings of the mind play tricks on us, making us believe that money is everything. Money has always been a by-product, that we earn based on our developed and developing skill sets that are in line with our purpose.

We fail to realize that love is never an attachment, and any attachment that we have with others is based on conditional love to fulfil our emotional needs because we are emotionally dependent on others. When we do not meet our emotional needs as adults, we repeat the same pattern of our childhood by depending on others to fulfil our emotional needs. We constantly seek comfort in others to make us feel emotionally secure and validate our actions and choices. As adults, it is our job to do that for ourselves.

To build a healthy relationship with our self, we need to allow all these issues to come to the surface and acknowledge them. We must slowly accept all parts of us, especially the part we choose to discard by not choosing authenticity and abandoning ourselves to please our caregiver and the societal structure. We must understand that everyone is on their individual journey, and there is a reason for an age gap between our caregivers and us. They are not going to be here forever, and neither are you.

If they had a positive impact on you, you can learn to see yourself through their eyes by imbibing those beliefs in yourself to be more authentic with time; that is how you keep their legacy alive, not by carrying the baton of a surname or choosing to play the role orchestrated or designed for you to fit a family setting made by the dogmatic societal structure to promote emotional dependency in adulthood with no authentic expression of individual self. These man-made rules and beliefs are the main reason many people continue to suffer.

You always have a choice to break out of this toxic loop that dictates how you should live your life by following the herd plan like everyone else or choosing to live your life on your terms and do things keeping your emotional well-being first as your duty towards self by taking accountability and responsibility for your own emotional needs.

Even if you follow the dogmatic societal plan, you will be emotionally, mentally, and financially responsible for everyone around you when you have not even evolved emotionally to hold that space for yourself in the first place. One will continue living in the same generational trauma as their caregivers. You will keep searching for meaning in this life by seeking validation for your existence and taking emotional responsibility for others instead of evolving emotionally in the first place.

We are always responsible for ourselves as adults before anyone else; we need to work on anything that keeps us from being the best version of our authentic selves by healing and validating our feelings. We heal by feeling the emotions trapped inside us, which we have not processed because we refuse to deal with them as grown-ups. Even if we journal how we think, it is more than enough to address what is bothering us or is trapped within us as an emotion; we can further narrow it down by talking about the incidents making us feel all those negative emotions that need to be addressed.

If someone's behaviour towards us makes us feel ashamed because we are feeling embarrassed about our actions, which led to the dissociation in the first place, we must understand that we are human beings first and are not here to achieve perfection on earth.

We are here to experience all the emotions the soul feels in human form available to us and, with time, to become comfortable with the range of emotions we have in our spectrum as a unique species. We need to, with age, identify the range of emotions that we have experienced until now; we need to, with time, identify our value system, which is ingrained as our belief within us i.e. loyalty, trustworthiness, giving, love, compassion, honesty, and so on.

Any time one of these values is compromised, or we are forced to compromise it in any situation, we are bound to react negatively because it goes against our ingrained value system as human beings. Our value systems make us who we are as humans; each of us is defined as a mix of these. Those with similar value systems tend to form friendships and stick with each other lifelong because of the shared value system that creates a natural bond and binds them freely for life due to it.

If one has to talk about the family unit of today, the world revolves around the provider of the family in terms of monetary contribution, as money is considered a basic need. Mostly, the one who has taken the responsibility to fulfil those needs sits at the top of the family chain of hierarchy. However, due to this imbalanced view of life, we attach more value to the provider of the dogmatic society and devalue our own lives based on where we land in the dogmatic societal structure. The role is already designed for us based on our gender; the part we have to play in this man-made family set-up. This leads to most family members finding meaning in mundane things, to fulfil each other's emotional dependency as a family, to attach meaning to our lives.

We see humans as gender first, which comes with pre-decided human values that are acceptable and not acceptable in the dogmatic societal structure. We fail to understand that we all have masculine traits such as leadership, assertiveness, boldness, or logic and feminine characteristics such as creativity, intuition, sensitivity, expressiveness, or nurturing. We cannot put ourselves in a psychological box and expect ourselves not to suffer.

When it comes to females in a dogmatic societal structure, most of them, once they have a child, lose their individuality by putting the child's needs above themselves, even after the child turns into an adult, by constantly self-abandoning themselves and not being authentic. It seems that with time, they have forgotten who they were, and they tend to like and do things their children do to make themselves content and happy.

These caregivers, primarily women in a patriarchal society, are conditioned or rather trained to play the role of a self-sacrificing mother based on societal structure, man-made religion, scriptures, and texts. The overall environment that they have been raised in complies with the same norm without any question or direction of individual expression of self as an identity; it was never her duty to be a full-time provider to the child; it was always an equal contribution in terms of time, will, and effort. Most females fail to realize the reason for their sufferings and constant state of being and acting in survival mode due to their conditioning based on self-abandonment, leading to disconnect from their authentic selves as adults.

A female is so much more than her reproductive organs; she deserves to be treated as equal to any man. Putting them in a box that puts them in survival mode and suits this man-made world through conditioning based on specific societally accepted ideas about motherhood, that is, being self-sacrificial, and a nurturer, caretaker, servant, labourer, cook, cleaner, etc.—we do not even give them a chance to find out what their authentic self is, let alone providing them with an equal opportunity to live an authentic life in the first place.

Women are constantly reminded by everyone in society of these beliefs; of marrying early because the right age would pass by, putting the man first, marrying someone who has status, and so on; it has created a psychological barrier about what a woman is supposed to be like. We have defined what it is to be a woman and what is societally considered a good one, by attaching our identities to it and accepting the well-defined role that is doomed for failure of the individual as a human being with no individuality.

Our emotions are involved in this false construct of belongingness based on the man-made societal structures so much so that many women, instead of breaking the generational trauma of such dogmatic societal structure, prepare and encourage their daughters to always do the domestic labour of the house just like her. At the same time, her son barely ever helps her with household work, be it cooking, cleaning, or washing. However, the son is always excused because he is the flag bearer of the family name and will carry their family legacy forward.

All this behaviour is tolerated and ignored, leading to so many men having the same entitled behaviour. They constantly look the other way from the sufferings of women in their home, let alone the outside world, because they love the attention and the privileges attached to their role in a patriarchal society. Even when they decide to say a word, they are well aware that they will have to do the household work along with the female members of their family. So they prefer to look the other way instead, hoping that his wife will be helping his mother and not work so much in the future. Such men are emotional toddlers in adult bodies who have not grown or even understood what patriarchy has done to women in the first place; such people are nothing but enablers of patriarchy.

Parents need to stop making women feel like liabilities in a patriarchal society if they are not married. This mindset silences millions of women and continues to harm them internally. Why objectify women as someone else's treasure from birth? Women should be free to choose their paths rather than being controlled by societal expectations of family honour.

Simultaneously, boys are pressured to suppress their emotions by being taught that vulnerability is weakness. This emotional repression contributes to crimes against women—rape, harassment, and abuse—fuelled by toxic societal norms. Men are conditioned to view women as possessions to acquire and bear children, rather than equal partners.

Marriage should not perpetuate outdated traditions that offer no true equality. Many men seek not partners but caretakers for their needs, refusing to evolve emotionally. Why is a woman expected to leave her home instead of a man? Why must she celebrate holidays with strangers whilst managing domestic chores, often contributing equally in the workplace?

Privileged men often cling to patriarchy, fearing that challenging it would require them to share domestic responsibilities. This perpetuates a toxic cycle, where women bear the burden of outdated expectations whilst men remain unprepared for true partnership.

We need to understand that being in the same family does not give anyone the right to shape the thinking of their children. We all should be provided with a safe space and enough freedom to create our own perceptions and views of the world surrounding us. Especially in patriarchal families, the unequal treatment of women, teaches us subconsciously that being a man makes us superior as a species. Ego drives men mostly in such a society, and they end up being the most toxic partners who fail to realize their role in promoting laws that promote such inequalities by abiding by them.

Be it asking women to dress in a certain way, change their home, name, or identity, expecting them to take care of them and their families by distributing household chores unequally, or expecting women to become members of their household by leaving theirs—such structures set up women for failure. They have to constantly deal with caregivers who are not theirs, enter motherhood due to societal pressure, leave jobs to fit their role of a perfect wife, tolerate a lot of disrespect, verbal and, at times, physical abuse because her own caregivers ask her to accept all of this because marriage means dealing with all this.

Women should always have a choice. Do not shame and blame them for choosing themselves and their self-respect if they walk out. Let us call it what it should be—a partnership on paper between two people, where both have the full right to walk out if it does not work. The need to control and marry according to religion, caste, creed, bank balance, looks, family's fortune, and the money that women's family can spend the marriage make the whole enterprise toxic.

True love is not based on this; it is between two people with shared values of love, understanding, care, respect, loyalty, trust, and mutual freedom to be authentic. It does not see religion, caste, creed, bank balance, family lineage, nations, only looks, or opinions of society. Love is free and should be based on emotional, mental, and physical compatibility between just two people who are equally invested in each other. Love yourself first, find your voice, and discover your authentic self before you seek love. Otherwise, you will always be trapped in this cycle of control by just following everyone in the herd!

Such structures were never based on emotional well-being and safety, which promote authenticity; they only encouraged emotional co-dependency between members of the families as they functioned as a joint unit that fulfilled each others' needs. Such family members rely heavily on external validation and continue to self-sacrifice their needs by continuously abandoning themselves to maintain harmony. Such family members see their children as an extension of themselves, and they continue to involve the kids with their friends, families, and relatives by asking them to sacrifice their time and attention to entertain them, with no choice based on how they feel around them.

However, coming back to the current system based on this man-made world, what happens is that everyone is assigned a role based on the man-made world according to their gender and their placement in the societal standing. As one ages, the baton of the same responsibilities is passed on. Mother, grandmother, grandparents, uncle, and aunts are assigned their roles, which decide family involvement. All the human values of empathy, kindness, love, selflessness, belongingness, and so on are given privileged treatment accordingly. The VIP pass of these values based on treatment in terms of behaviour and actions are given to the immediate offspring, and they, with some boundaries, are provided to the rest depending on their situation and lifestyle.

In a patriarchal society, women are treated as someone else's money, a responsibility, if born in a family, nation, or community that follows this structure. The caregivers' primary responsibility towards their daughters is to raise them right by providing them with education and moral values of being a domesticated person who is submissive, agreeable, knows all the domestic chores, and always puts others' needs first. They are groomed on the same lines as their mothers, so they can be married into a good family and produce their offspring.

For a girl's marriage, the groom is searched based on their educational qualification, societal standing, religious beliefs, purchasing power, worldly achievements, etc. What happens due to the dogma of societal structure like this is that the roles are assigned by birth, based on gender. The man of the house usually becomes the self-appointed dictator of the house, who is considered an idol, as he has taken the financial responsibility to provide for everyone in the house; no one questions why the females have never been offered an equal opportunity to decide for themselves.

Due to this, the lives of everyone in the family set-up revolve around the one holding the financial power or taking the role of a provider most of the time. Girls are considered an additional responsibility of the family. They need to be married off to a respectable family, where they can produce offspring to carry the baton of that family. The parents do everything to make their daughter the most eligible bachelorette and the most prized possession, that will have enough men who want her hand for marriage. They raise them by educating them, teaching them all domestic chores, and ensuring that they are proper in size and colour as per their perception of the ideal body.

Further, when she ages and reaches the 'ripe of marriage,' she is objectified as a fruit to be married off so that she can produce offspring after her education. If she is allowed to work (often, this is to get someone with a good bank balance and family name), the groom is searched for just like shopping, offline (through their communities) or online (through marriage apps), based on a man-made system of religion, family name, purchasing power, qualification, job or business, material wealth, etc.

Most of the time, such families do not even teach their children emotional independence as that remains their ticket to be constantly involved in the decision-making of their children's lives, and they find a purpose in living through their kids. They always see their kids as extensions of themselves and feel that they have earned the authority by raising them to dictate their children's actions, behaviour, and needs in the first place, by setting the course of their lives.

Such kids never grow up emotionally and always consult their parents for all their significant decisions. When they become adults, kids of such parents lack self-worth, trust, and confidence and have people-pleasing tendencies. They often turn precisely like their parents to please them without having their authentic personality. Such parents' intentions might be to protect their children from the harm of the world. Still, they fail to realize that such a need for control can be detrimental as you cannot always protect your kids from everyone and they will not be in their lives until the end of time; that is why the age gap exists.

The best thing one can do is give their children emotionally a safe space to make mistakes and develop a healthy relationship with themselves. Once they do that, they can be the most authentic version of themselves, who will be emotionally independent and look after themselves ideally once they leave the earth. This immediate solution to save such children will cause them a lot of suffering in their future, as adults as they continue to be emotionally dependent on their parents, to decide for them, as their sense of judgement has not been formed yet, even as adults. This overprotectiveness is detrimental to their emotional health as adults, as they continue to be toddlers who do not know how to regulate their own emotions independently.

Such conditional love of such parents or family set-up is binding due to the imbalance created by the dogma of societal structure in the first place. We are not taught to be emotionally independent as individuals. We would stop needing each other to keep the dogmatical societal structure of a family unit based on surname, nationality, belief, religion, caste, creed, culture, and colour by creating offspring to keep the baton running. Such love and hierarchy are based on attachment, and we need to understand that attachment is the root cause of suffering.

We need to question ourselves: why, as adults, are we still emotionally dependent on our caregivers, relatives, friends, and family around us to take care of our emotional needs? Deep down, it is rooted in our fear-based mentality based on abandonment, rejection, not being good enough or lack of self-worth, lack of emotional safety from within, lack of self-trust, lack of self-confidence, etc.

The emotional dependency on the family is due to our inability to form a secure attachment within ourselves, as a daily reminder to ourselves that we are loved and cared for. It gives us a false sense of belongingness that puts us in a box, where our human values of love, kindness, selflessness, empathy, care, and belongingness are reserved for them before anyone else. However, we need to realize that their behaviour is based on unfulfilled emotional needs, and once they are fulfilled, it will bring change accordingly in their actions and behaviour.

Chapter 4
The Purpose of our Existence

The deeper we flow with our lives, the more we eventually understand our purpose as humans, which is simply to be here. The chance of existing, living, and breathing is nothing short of a miracle. This is why we are here: to continue being our childlike selves, never taking life too seriously, always finding lessons and joy in whatever we experience, and exploring this wonderful life by being fully alive. It is about seeing life all around you through different lenses. We feel short-term happiness and gratification when we buy artificial things to tick the checklist designed by the dogmatic societal structure.

We serve different purposes but exist in various shapes and forms. We are in separate cycles of life doing our part: trees change with the seasons and bloom simultaneously; land and rivers hold all the goodness, shifting their courses through calamities, droughts, storms, and rains; animals survive by hunting, fighting, and protecting while maintaining the ecosystem by simply being alive. The art of noticing life in motion reminds us that we are all in different forms—balancing, existing, living, and breathing as part of nature—and going through phases of the journey while serving the purpose that binds us together on a living planet called "EARTH." An interesting fact: EARTH rearranged is HEART; you can see how poetically interconnected we are. Tell me something more beautiful than this that has ever existed. That's why our existence has always been a blessing. We are all one, held together by a living planet. We should be grateful for being alive on this earth that keeps everything in motion so we can coexist in diverse forms.

The choices one makes, if they harm another living being or cause suffering due to selfish motives or inconsideration, cannot have good intentions for the betterment of living creatures. Lack of empathy leads us to opt for such choices that conflict with our fundamental human values. Until we stop making choices from survival mode, we will operate out of ego, constantly concerned with our self-image—that is, how others perceive us. Our actions will be driven by the fear of survival and the fear of not being accepted, imposed by societal conditioning, rules, and ways of living. We feed our egoistic selves as long as we choose to be followers, never prioritising our emotional needs and authentic selves.

Throughout history, anything that caused division among humans separated them from their core values of love, kindness, empathy, and compassion. The dogmatic man-made societal structure is the foundation and root cause of our suffering, programming our internal belief system with an artificial idea of what it means to be human. These stories carried agendas to separate people so they could be divided and ruled over, turning them into followers rather than leaders of their own lives, erecting psychological barriers instead of fostering connection among humanity in this man-made world.

Societal conditioning has created a divide between humans and their natural state by creating belief systems by conditioning and programming minds based on nation, gender, colour, creed, money, brands, family, relatives, religion, cultural beliefs, purchasing power, entertainment figures, celebrity worship, caste systems, gender differentiation, and spiritual cults. These structures place us in separate psychological boxes, assigning roles we are born to play, following a 'happily ever after' plan as a herd globally. This keeps humanity in survival mode, driven by animalistic instincts, making choices that contradict the innate human value system we were born with, disconnected from authentic selves and the thriving mode of living from the heart.

Dictators are not only figures like Hitler; anyone who dictates how you feel through their actions has power over you. This power stems from emotional dependency and expectations that they would act as you would. Families often mimic governments: some adopt democratic decisions that consider feelings, while many are ruled by dictatorship, where parents feel entitled to make final calls on their children's major life choices—schools, university courses, careers, spouses, children's names—regardless of age. Such parents see their children as extensions of themselves and their family name, perpetuating generational trauma without realizing that it is a man-made construct. They always have the choice to break this cycle and allow children to become their own people, forming judgements and building lives on their terms. This may require shedding mental and social identities such as surname, religion, nationality, or caste.

Today's dictators often include parents who fail to respect free will. We were freer centuries ago with singular monarchs than many adults enslaved by parental control now. Few understand the importance of free will, yet as adults, we hold the right to exercise it every day.

Intellect is not merely acquiring book knowledge; natural intellect is the wisdom of life that expands knowledge and keeps us seekers of truth based on internal human values. Rejecting the dogmatic societal game of survival of the fittest, where everyone loses, frees us to be fully alive inside, emotionally independent, and authentic.

The reasons behind whom a person marries tell much about their emotional maturity. When parents decide their adult children's spouses, it shows that those children lack emotional independence and have never learnt to make important decisions without parental input. These adults remain emotionally adolescent, dependent on others for validation, their emotional age locked as teenagers who will never evolve. They continue generational trauma by passing emotional dependence to the next generation, causing ongoing suffering from draining, harmful societal rules, blindly followed because "that's how it's done." This results in a tragic loss of diverse cultural celebration—culture reduced to dominance rather than connection. Culture should be a choice: adopting what aligns with our core humanity and rejecting anything that undermines our fundamental rights to be human, including emotional independence.

The only hold others have over us is emotional investment or dependence for our emotional needs. That is why everything functions as it does. When we decide enough is enough and choose conscious emotional regulation and validation, those who once exploited us crumble like a house of cards. By learning self-regulation and creating emotionally safe spaces within ourselves to be and act authentically, we break generational trauma and expose emotional immaturity disguised as adult behaviour. These emotional teenagers are often narcissists.

First, we must understand that, as adults, we are solely responsible for our behaviour and emotions—how we feel about people, situations, and our environment. We are responsible for ourselves alone. It is not our parents' job to determine our profession, spouse, home, or family plans. If we remain emotionally dependent on our parents, both parties share blame—parents for failing to define life purpose clearly and adults for not evolving emotionally. We are here to learn independently. Consulting parents is valuable, but emotional independence is the goal. Parents should teach emotional regulation skills, not manage emotions for us. Without this, people-pleasing develops, and we care more about others' opinions than our own authenticity.

Our attachment patterns, especially with the parent of the opposite sex, often breed anxious or avoidant tendencies. We seek approval from that parent, using people-pleasing to validate our life choices. The more we please others, the more we abandon ourselves, neglecting our emotional needs, safety, trust, and comfort. This fosters a self-sacrificing martyr persona that maintains family harmony but costs our authenticity.

Anyone seeking perfection—be it body, weight, looks, work, or food—is ruled by ego in survival mode, continually self-critical and negative. Their ego governs them, driven by others' perceptions, because internally, they view themselves with hostility and require external validation to feel worthy.

The dogmatic societal structure thrives on such emotional dependency, feeding followers who consume entertainment and celebrity culture as distractions for emotional regulation. They remain disconnected from their true feelings, never experiencing authentic self-awareness.

People at war with themselves are not the ones to seek support from in our pursuit of peace. Their mental cages keep them trapped, and relying on them for solace wastes our time and energy. Time is our finite currency—spending it wisely means being the main character in your own story, unapologetically authentic before the world tries to mould you into a follower or transient survivor according to dogmatic societal games of control.

It is our duty as adults to validate and regulate our emotional state. Emotions transcend gender, felt equally by all humans. Dividing emotional roles by gender causes widespread suffering. Men are permitted anger and passion; women, expression and vulnerability—when roles reverse, discomfort arises. We are never taught to embrace the full range of emotions regardless of gender or to become adults who validate all feelings, whether good, bad, or ugly. Loving, accepting, and validating all parts of ourselves is our superpower. Self-perception remains the most critical parameter keeping us aligned with authenticity.

We are here to experience all human emotions and create emotional safety within ourselves.

The goal of life is not merely to survive but to exist and thrive. We become ensnared in a man-made, unspoken rulebook: school, college, work, marriage, children, retirement, all while accumulating and hoarding wealth, ensuring entertainment along the way with a checklist of possessions and social markers. We lose sight of the purpose of existence—life itself. Being alive, free from illness, safe, with food and shelter, is a blessing worthy of gratitude. Instead of appreciating this, we fixate on what we lack, staying trapped in survival mode. We are exactly where we need to be, and gratitude—the language of the heart—nudges us from survival to thriving, as we were always meant to live.

When recalling past relationship pain, understand it was never love but attachment based on emotional dependency—seeking externally what we lacked inside. Doubts we replay stem from fear, yet love has always been within, waiting to be found. The recurring fears arise from attachment to relationships where the other person did not meet our emotional needs. Conditioning forced us to seek love externally rather than cultivate it within.

Our lack of inner emotional support, wounds from self-abandonment, and emotional dependency push us to constantly seek others in love's name. Yet this desire is attachment rooted in dependency. You cannot accept real love without first loving yourself. Emotional depth is your currency—we attract or repel what we hold inside. What we call "love" often masks attachment to dopamine, serotonin, and oxytocin derived from others, a false security grounded in man-made structures of relationships, societies, families, and religions.

In the past, your attachment and connection caused pain because your emotional needs were unmet or you felt unsafe to voice them, focused instead on making others feel secure. Recognize your part in this cycle. We have subjected ourselves repeatedly to trauma under cultural myths of love, rather than embracing self-acceptance. We lived the same tragic narratives, believing ourselves unlovable, never realising we deserved love.

That is why we crave love; we must give it to ourselves first, reminding ourselves we are worthy. Searching externally leaves us lost when love's supply is cut off. Love frees; attachment binds and causes suffering. Understanding this is key: your journey has always been yours alone. You are the main character in a love story—a return to your authentic self, the director of your own production.

Recognize this individual journey. Our role is not to carry others' emotional burdens but to guide and support them kindly. We cannot save anyone—not even loved ones. Their growth is their own journey. We can be guides and friends offering suggestions but cannot shield them from necessary lessons or pain they must undergo to mature emotionally.

Free will allows each person to judge for themself and grow. Life's fragility reminds us to wish for our loved ones' independence and resilience, even if we are absent in hardship.

The saviour complex must be relinquished. Though the desire to prevent others' suffering is noble, we cannot save everyone all the time. People must learn through life's full spectrum of experiences—good, bad, and ugly—to make their own best choices.

Every adult is responsible for their own emotional health, just as you are. We cannot bear others' emotional responsibility; our support lies in standing by them during turmoil, not dictating life paths. People seek companionship, not control.

Judgement is the worst gift—always keep an open mind, strive to understand others' pain and stories, and recognize what shapes their actions. Even if their actions clash with our values, consider their emotional turmoil and how survival mode alters priorities toward coping, often at the expense of consideration. Fear and ego fuel decisions, aided by illusions of the mind, justified by past experiences, to avoid vulnerability.

We are not here to please others for validation or to be marionettes in the family or embody societal roles built on martyrdom, dictatorship, or self-sacrifice to remain relevant. We are here for independent living, honouring the gift of life through authentic, emotionally independent living aligned with our purpose, rather than following herd plans.

We are human first—sharing values and emotions equally—gender comes second, and relationship labels follow.

Authenticity is not rebellion but fidelity to one's truths amid external pressure. Loved ones who support us despite disagreement maintain genuine bonds. We lose only connections based on attachment where people depended on us to fill loneliness, fears of abandonment or rejection or worthlessness.

Many caregivers sought control to feel emotionally safe, but that burden was never ours to carry. Their emotional responsibility belongs to them; their refusal to heal is no excuse for self-abandonment.

If caregivers truly love you, they will come around in time; if not, you were but an extension of their expectations. They failed to see you individually, viewing you only as family legacy. You owe nothing for having been born into their family. Beyond adulthood, you have the right to live on your terms, set boundaries, and care for those who respect your emotional security.

You are not here to follow others. Remember, we lead our own lives, deciding terms for ourselves without external influence. If guilt arises, know you are a work in progress, learning to prioritize your emotional needs. Choosing authenticity takes time but it is the path to freedom, by breaking cycles born of dogmatic societal conditioning.

One day at a time, build inner confidence until validation from others is no longer necessary. This is how we break generational trauma and end widespread suffering—by learning to validate and love ourselves.

By accepting others as they are and respecting that change requires their own readiness, we recognize that trauma cannot be broken collectively but must be approached individually. Like us, others believe they know what is best for themselves, and that must be honoured—even if their choices cause suffering.

We cannot change those who lack self-awareness; some may be so entrenched in external validation that change seems impossible. Particularly caregivers with deep wounds crave validation long denied, often through status or wealth displays.

Helping them requires boundaries, offering emotional safety without assuming their wounds. Acting as guides of authenticity and acceptance benefits both. Validation they seek externally can, over time, be nurtured from within.

Many of us fear vulnerability because of unhealed emotional wounds and attachment issues from childhood, forming avoidant, anxious, or dismissive patterns. We want rescuers instead of recognising our job as adults to heal ourselves.

Modern relationships often mimic this dynamic: runners avoid emotions and themselves; chasers seek validation externally, longing for an idealised love to prove worth. Both are emotionally unavailable, trapped in cycles repeating childhood emotional dependencies by unconsciously choosing similar partners. Both blame others for their hurt, unaware that their emotional dependence fuels the cycle.

We must let go of those who no longer serve our emotional growth, regardless of ties of friendship or family. Clutter extends beyond material possessions; emotional clutter affects internal well-being. Just as we are mindful of financial investments, we must carefully choose where and with whom we invest our emotional energy.

Exposing ourselves repeatedly to unhealed emotional toddlers perpetuates suffering, influenced by our internal environment. Humans are creatures of habit, absorbing attitudes as children. As adults, we have the choice to leave environments that keep us stuck in survival mode due to others' wounds, reclaiming responsibility for our own emotional health.

Declutter your environment to change your reality. Until you provide your inner child with emotional safety and space to reconnect with your authentic self, enabling emotional growth and healthy self-relationship, you will continue suffering the same issues, faced with familiar but different faces—reflections of your own unhealed emotional state, borrowed and projected from caregivers.

Chapter 5

The Perception of Self and the World Around us

People are often more concerned about how others perceive them than anything else, especially regarding their societal standing. To prove they are enough, many will go the extra mile, even overboard, in their actions to shape others' perceptions. For such individuals, the need to be liked surpasses the need to be loved. Once their needs are met through you, their affection shifts at their convenience. This behaviour can be observed in close family, friends, relatives, and community alike. Instead of taking it personally, understand that those living in survival mode, burdened by unhealed emotions, fulfil their emotional needs through external validation. How others perceive them becomes more important than embodying true values or character. This distinction helps differentiate authenticity from attachment.

Genuine people uphold human values consistently, as their character reflects their truth and remains in harmony with who they are. They neither pretend nor hide; without any image to maintain, their minds are free from concern over others' opinions. They enjoy solitude and their own company, speak the truth, treat others equally, and practice unconditional empathy. Conversely, those fixated on maintaining an image of kindness, generosity, or self-sacrifice display affection selectively, responding only while their emotional needs are met and dependency remains. Once their needs fade, their actions reveal that you are no longer important. Such love is conditioned by convenience and emotional dependency, driven by a desire to be seen as caring and compassionate both socially and personally.

Not everyone can love freely or without conditions, and that is acceptable—such behaviour reflects how deeply they love themselves. These individuals rely constantly on external validation to be liked and loved because they lack internal self-love. They seek to control others' perceptions to feel needed, worthy, validated, and emotionally safe. Often, they are unaware of their emotional wounds and unable to heal or grow because of this blindness. Not everyone is considerate, but rather they are living in survival mode, caught in emotional immaturity, regardless of age. Such adults are 'emotional toddlers with grey hair,' lacking inner wisdom.

We must see people for who they truly are, not who we wish them to be. This understanding grants better perspective—not only of others but also of ourselves—highlighting what to avoid to prevent suffering and how to learn from our mistakes. More importantly, it frees us from the burden of expecting love or validation from them. People will continue behaving according to how the world perceives them, prioritizing image over genuine self-love.

Everyone carries good, bad, and ugly traits, whether we accept them or not. Failing to accept ourselves and persisting in projecting a tailored, false image for external validation to fulfil emotional needs is far worse. Such denial guarantees continued suffering.

Accepting that many are heavily conditioned and programmed by dogmatic societal beliefs releases us from the expectation of being loved authentically by them. Over time, we may develop compassion for those caught in such lifelong societal dramas—those who have forgotten they are the main characters of their own lives. Instead of controlling others, they could reclaim the driver's seat to heal emotional wounds and connect with their authentic selves, rather than abandoning themselves to please others by maintaining false images.

Much of dogmatic societal structure is founded on a false sense of belonging, built on external validation and emotional co-dependency through attachments. This man-made construct fuels ongoing suffering. It was never designed to promote emotional well-being, safety, or authenticity but merely to encourage emotional co-dependency among family units fulfilling each other's needs in a cycle of dependency.

Such individuals often do not know how to meet emotional needs beyond their immediate 'herd' or family bubble. They tend to live their emotional experiences, positive or negative, solely within this societal framework.

Children raised in such families often grow into adults struggling with self-confidence, authenticity, self-worth, and self-respect. Overprotective caregivers see them as extensions of themselves and fail to provide the emotional safety necessary for independence. Though protective in intent, these parents inhibit their children's growth, leaving them unable to think independently. Even minor decisions—from going out to taking a vacation—require parental validation.

The age gap is irrelevant; the parents' need to feel needed blinds them to the harm their control inflicts. Such parents are emotionally wounded themselves, driven by fears and control needs that cause lasting damage. Excessive control prevents children from becoming emotionally independent adults. This selfish parenting resembles a wolf in sheep's clothing—appearing caring but causing profound long-term harm.

These parents fear abandonment and maintain control to ensure they remain indispensable for emotional reassurance. Their children must learn to trust their own judgement by developing an emotionally healthy self-relationship. Unfortunately, fears and conditional beliefs are transferred to children who then remain trapped in inherited emotional wounds, repeating generational trauma under the guise of conditional love.

Such caregivers never embraced authentic life; their dependence on external validation hinders emotional growth and keeps them in survival mode. They constantly involve children in family networks, demanding time and attention to sustain their emotional needs. Children, however, should have the freedom to express feelings, make choices, and establish relationships based on their own perceptions of emotional safety.

This does not mean one should reject family bonds. Families founded on human values—empathy, kindness, love, selflessness, compassion—where fear, abandonment, rejection, and low self-worth do not govern relationships—allow free will. Individuals grow by making independent choices founded on experience and introspection, shedding fear and ego that trap others in survival mode, validation seeking, and constant approval needs from family, society, or social media.

Chapter 6

Entering Your Thriving Era

The world we live in is a realm dominated by popularity and the pursuit of perfection. Globally famous individuals achieve popularity by selling us the euphoria of 'happy hormones,' becoming the living symbols of success—largely defined by wealth. Their role is to personify success, linking it to feelings of happiness, authority, fame, money, love, and contentment. We idolize them, aspire to emulate their lives, and grant them power over us by becoming followers, especially in the age of social media, where we are relentlessly exposed to them via marketing, branding, and advertising.

Their aim is to saturate our vision, presenting themselves as live influencers or cultural icons demanding worship, so we continuously associate them with all the happy feelings that define success. Yet instead of practising gratitude, empathy, or giving back to society, many become insatiable money hoarders, blinded by power, fame, and material gain.

Regardless of their wealth, their sole desire is to be worshipped alive—narcissists driven by hunger for authority, money, and fame. Such individuals are profoundly selfish and egocentric, existing mainly to feed their egos by increasing follower counts.

This model is replicated by countless others who waste Earth's resources promoting fast fashion, human exploitation, and consumption of harmful, chemical-laden products. Such imbalances in the dogmatic societal structure thrive because money grants power, authority, and control over the masses. Why, then, do we fail to unite against this idol-worshipping, money-hoarding culture? Because those in power control our emotions. For thousands of years, humanity possessed skills to grow food, sew clothes, heal with herbs, build homes, and survive independently. Yet in two generations, these skills have almost vanished, leaving us utterly dependent on the systems created by this dogmatic societal structure.

They exert control through public figures, corporations, brands, and imagery. We empower them by giving our undivided attention, time, and becoming their followers—consuming curated content and accepting white lies—thereby ceasing to question their power amassed through money hoarding, exploitation, lack of transparency in tax usage, and business practices.

The entire struggle within this dogmatic societal structure centres on ownership. Countries fight for land, humans for property and relationships, aiming always to own people, places, or things. The system sets us up for failure by teaching survival, not human betterment, keeping us in fight-or-flight mode and primitive hierarchies based on money, gender, colour, country, profession, and bank balance.

We have become FMCG consumers, unaware of where plastics, clothes, and food waste go after 'recycling.' Are these firms legitimate? Do we stop and purchase responsibly or acknowledge our duty towards the environment? Questioning and taking responsibility for our consumption is vital.

Take that control back. Fear of the unknown fuels this system that money hoarders exploit. True change arises when we refuse to succumb to adversity and instead learn lost skills, expanding financial independence and reducing reliance on others for physical, emotional, and financial needs.

In our quest for perfection, we not only chase checklists—college, career, marriage, children, retirement—but also external appearances. Society judges us by looks, ignoring the internal self. Schools teach only one male and female body type, neglecting natural diversity, fostering insecurities essential for societal division and control. This manufactured insecurity sustains the system, preventing us from addressing real human suffering and evolutionary progress.

Division and control through dogmatic societal structures enforce survival mode, preventing us thriving by acting against human values. Money hoarders maintain unjust dominance, flaunting superiority through social media, exacerbating inequalities.

Emotionally unavailable people cannot offer emotional availability, whether in relationships, family, or friendship. Those trapped in survival mode lack love, care, and compassion—they cannot provide what they themselves lack. They live within illusions of perfection and exclude anyone imperfect, failing to recognize that our humanity lies precisely in our imperfections.

Perfectionism is a social construct designed to ensure failure and prevent human thriving. A person in thriving mode empathizes naturally, free from ego or the popularity chase built on materialistic versions of Maslow's hierarchy of needs.

This understanding helps release resentment, hurt, and unrealistic expectations placed on others for emotional support. As adults, the most powerful act is taking accountability and responsibility for our own lives and emotions. This does not negate the value of support systems but stresses self-reliance. When able to regulate our emotions, we seek companionship rather than dependence. Authentic relationships are rooted in true connection rather than fear of abandonment.

Inability to be alone or maintain healthy self-relationships leads to meaningless connections that lack mutual growth. Fear of losing others must not overshadow fear of losing oneself in futile people-pleasing. We exist to discover ourselves and embrace our unique life path, living fully in the present moment. Anything or anyone robbing your peace must be removed without hesitation. You are the protagonist of your life; own it unapologetically today.

Happiness is not a product of money; money only offers fleeting gratification, keeping us trapped in survival confusion. Society teaches us to chase happiness, but true contentment is life's goal. Happiness is one emotion among many—anger, grief, joy, and more. Pursuing one at the expense of others is a losing game.

Many live bitter lives, feeling others' suffering as cosmic justice, unaware they hold the power to change their own worlds. That empowerment can inspire widespread goodness. Your worth is not tied to money or social roles—husband, wife, parent, friend—these are labels, not essence.

In any situation, ask yourself, "What can I do about it?" If powerless, acceptance is crucial for mental well-being. True surrender means reclaiming power by prioritising mental health.

Emotionally unavailable people cannot validate us; unconditional love for others starts with unconditional self-love. What we give ourselves reflects outwardly.

If we are self-critical, the world seems critical; our inner narrative shapes external reality. Positive affirmations align us with the heart's wisdom, while fear binds us to survival mode's reactive mindset.

We label some as energy vampires without understanding their pain—they seek externally what they lack internally. Many crave fame, money, and power because they do not love themselves. Our hearts speak gratitude; without hope, depression ensues. Hope for tomorrow sustains us amidst toxicity.

Growth and change are ladders out of survival mode. We must shed emotional dependency and self-abandonment to rediscover authenticity and emotional independence. The conscious mind, like a search engine, pulls up countless negative thoughts based on past experiences and self-perception, trapping us in fight-or-flight cycles sustained by man-made conditioning.

Our emotions respond psychologically to these internal narratives, programming behaviour, thoughts, and identity. When our emotional needs are unmet, and self-worth, confidence, and trust are low, disconnection from authenticity intensifies. Perfectionism arises from ego, fueling survival stress and keeping us dependent on others, granting them power over us.

Attachment to man-made roles—job titles, money, possessions—falsely defines our identities, imprisoning us in invisible psychological boxes. We must accept this reality as the root of our suffering, which sustains external validation cycles, sacrificing our precious time and emotional currency on attachments and people incapable of meeting our needs.

Perfectionism is an ego-driven mirage, underpinned by self-abandonment and people-pleasing, aimed at gaining acceptance and love. It masks internal insecurity and prevents authentic living.

Those who seek perfection in body, work, or other areas often have fraught relationships with themselves, ruled by ego and external perceptions. Such people harbour negativity internally and depend on others for validation, remaining disconnected from their true selves.

The dogmatic societal structure thrives on such emotional dependence. These individuals consume entertainment and celebrity culture obsessively, needing distractions to regulate emotions through others, lacking true self-awareness.

To enter thriving mode, we must learn self-love and practise it daily, becoming the main character in our own stories. This requires unlearning societal conditioning and removing limiting beliefs. People meet us only at the level they meet themselves; those emotionally unavailable will not understand us. Blame is unproductive; instead, cultivate empathy for those who struggle to show up even for themselves.

Many live sad, dependent lives shaped by negative self-perception and perpetual emotional reliance. These internal prisons breed torment; those trapped cannot endure solitude and escape into distraction.

People at war with themselves are not sources of peace. Their mental cages keep them suffering in survival mode. Seeking their validation wastes your energy. Time is your currency—spend it wisely as the lead in your life story. Be unapologetically yourself before others attempt to mould you as a mere follower within dogmatic, survival-driven societal roles.

Chapter 7
Choosing Authenticity Over Everything Else

If choosing your authentic self leads to conflict with others, even your loved ones, have the courage to pick yourself every single time, even if it means parenting yourself out of guilt, shame, and helplessness for your emotional growth and healing. This is how our relationship with our self becomes destroyed, through constant self-abandonment due to self-sacrificing behaviour and failing to prioritize our emotional needs. Conflicts can be viewed from a different perspective as alternative ways of thinking, feeling, and acting in situations that life presents. We all act according to our emotions, and that is acceptable. When disagreement arises, we always have the choice to listen to all viewpoints and act in a way we deem right or aligns with our genuine feelings about the situation.

Those who truly love you will always love your authentic self; those who shower you with conditional love and affection to meet their emotional needs love you based on their convenience. Their behaviour shifts at will and has nothing to do with who you are. Losing them is actually a sign of removing emotionally unhealthy attachments from your life. This will not be considered a loss in the long run once you begin living authentically and becoming emotionally independent with a healthy, regulated nervous system that no longer operates in survival mode.

People who genuinely love you for who you are, without conditions, will always provide you with a emotionally safe space to be yourself. You no longer have to abandon yourself or sacrifice your emotional needs to earn their love. You can be your true, authentic self in their presence, and they will love you as a whole person. They will never place you in a box of judgement and will always support you and your choices, even when they disagree with your perspective.

When we choose to operate from our heart space and listen to our intuition, we can begin building a healthy relationship with our inner child and emotionally connect with ourselves. We need to understand that all the psychological pressure we felt—created in our heads due to conditional beliefs we associated with our identity—was merely a projection from our caregivers of who we are, combined with societally predetermined roles we were supposed to play based on gender rather than human values. This served to perpetuate the dogmatic societal family structure.

It was never based on who we are inside, without gender, as human beings. It was a projection of conditioned cultural beliefs from a dogmatic societal structure designed to make us fit roles created before we were even born into a man-made family setup. It has nothing to do with who we are as human beings internally, but everything to do with the responsibilities, expectations, and behaviours attached to gender roles in a dogmatic societal structure.

We are enough and were always enough as human beings, with all the tools ingrained within us to build our character. We never had to prove our worth to anyone by enduring psychological examinations in our heads to fit preassigned roles in dogmatic societal structures, sacrificing our authenticity in ways that only promote self-abandonment and emotional co-dependency.

We can consciously choose to operate from ego based on our fears as a mask to feel emotionally safe, which keeps us constantly in survival mode. We need to remove the psychological pressure of carrying others' emotional responsibility in the form of expectations assigned to us based on gender. The moment we understand that had we been born a different gender, the pressure to be perfect based on marks, university, careers, and family roles would not have been assigned to us, we realize the special treatment was based on gender, not humanity.

All this pressure to live up to expectations has created an inner critical voice demanding perfection. We tend to carve our identities based on dogmatic societal structures because we have attached our self-worth and identities to external things, constantly leading us to seek external validation and acceptance from dogmatic societal structures that promise a false sense of belonging.

Always remember: you can only give others what you possess and meet them at the level of your emotional development. If you love yourself conditionally, you will always love others conditionally based on fears and emotional dependency, never freely. You will continue making adult choices based on attachments due to emotional dependency and will continue seeking love from others to feel emotionally fulfilled, secure, safe, and complete—as continues to be sold by dogmatic societal structures as a framework of false human belonging, making everyone follow the same script of 'happily ever after' by creating families as status symbols of 'making it in life.'

The more authentic we become, the more connected we become with our inner emotional selves. Love is our language without conditioning or attachment due to emotional dependency. To love another without attachment or emotional co-dependency is the purest, most selfless, and authentic love one can give. That's why we feel like ourselves in the company of nature, where we are accepted entirely for our authenticity. We feel emotionally safe and complete because we have always been part of nature, not vice versa.

We need to speak the language of love as humankind, straight from the heart. This doesn't mean avoiding boundaries with people who constantly disrespect or discredit us as humans. Disrespect isn't only shouting but also being inconsiderate towards another living being, including humans, which can be felt in small actions. How much consideration someone shows us and how they make us feel is always reflected through their actions, behaviour, and reactions after their emotional needs are fulfilled and they no longer need us emotionally. That's when people with high narcissistic tendencies drop their masks, because they are only capable of conditional self-love, which reflects in their external world.

Being empathetic in today's world is your superpower. The only way to protect yourself from narcissists is to observe how they narrate their life stories and speak about people, even if they are your caregivers. Detach from everything surrounding you and notice if the caregiver constantly blames others by playing victim and martyr roles, maintains many superficial friendships, obsesses over materialistic achievements and ownership of people and things, displays grandiose self-perception, constantly gossips, promotes emotional co-dependency in adult children by being involved in everyday decision-making, forces family to entertain their changing preferences, views people and the world in black and white terms, and dictates how others should live.

They are always driven by ego and fear; they care only about their image and what others think, and cannot tolerate being disliked. It's all about maintaining appearances; their family and friends serve as PR for their greatness. Such people lack depth, character, and authenticity—their actions, behaviour, and personalities change like seasons depending on life situations. They see people as extensions of themselves or objects for emotional use. Their love will always be conditional because they fear abandonment; they cannot be alone and hate their own company.

Their need to control everyone stems from childhood wounds of emotional insecurity. They control family and friends by making them emotionally codependent so they can never think, feel, or become emotionally independent, ensuring continued need for the narcissist to fulfil their emotional needs. Their drama and narratives about themselves change conveniently. Hold on—the truth eventually catches up with such drama queens and kings who thrive in chaos and feel no remorse about hurting others whilst creating their man-made kingdoms of worldly possessions.

Change your inner voice to one based on human values: love, compassion, empathy, care, forgiveness, selflessness, and so forth. This will help you become best friends with your inner child. Your inner child will, with time, learn to trust you as you consistently choose authenticity over self-abandonment. Your inner reality will slowly reflect self-confidence, trust, compassion, love, forgiveness, care, and authenticity. You will understand that love is always free, and once we learn to love ourselves unconditionally, only then can we do the same for others.

Gratitude is the language of the heart—practise it consistently to build a relationship with yourself and begin the journey of emotional growth until you love yourself unconditionally, enabling you to love everyone equally, freely, and unconditionally as human beings and all living creatures. That is the purpose of our existence: to become the best version of ourselves based on human values, making them part of our inner world so they reflect in our external world without societal conditioning and limiting beliefs.

We must learn to forgive ourselves for being human. Growth comes with mistakes, emotional highs and lows, and moments we wish we could undo. Expressing ourselves—sometimes imperfectly—is part of the journey. Shame has no place in healing; instead, we need compassion, especially for ourselves. Emotional regulation is not innate—it's a learned process. We stumble, bottle things up, or lash out before understanding what we're feeling. That doesn't make us broken; it makes us human. Apologising when we've caused harm matters, but so does self-forgiveness, even when the other person is no longer around. If they truly cared, they would want peace for you too.

We often abandon our authentic selves to meet others' expectations. When we prioritize external validation or societal norms over inner truth, we remain trapped in cycles of suffering. Real healing begins when we take responsibility for our emotions and stop outsourcing our worth. Only then can we create a space where our inner child feels safe and seen.

The parts of ourselves we dislike are often those we've rejected to survive. These parts deserve acceptance, not judgement. Healing means reprogramming our inner voice with compassion, instead of criticism, and embracing all aspects of who we are. We owe no one—family or otherwise—continued access to our lives if the relationship keeps us in survival mode. Emotional safety is not a luxury; it's a necessity. You are not obligated to shrink yourself to meet the expectations of those who refuse to grow.

True connection isn't built on roles or expectations—it's built on authenticity. Few will love you for who you are, not who you perform to be. Let go of the need to be liked; it's often rooted in childhood fear, not truth. By healing that fear, we end generational cycles of pain and create new patterns rooted in self-trust and emotional independence.

Forgiveness doesn't mean approval; it means choosing peace. People's behaviour reflects their inner wounds, not your worth. Set boundaries, release the need to fix or prove, and let go. You were never responsible for healing others. You were only ever responsible for choosing yourself.

Until we continue carrying the emotional baggage of insecurities based on our fears, we will always live in survival mode, preferring to play it safe due to emotionally co-dependent tendencies rooted in fears, insecurities, and abandonment issues. Life is an unknown territory—your playground filled with bumpy and smooth rides—but you need to remove the blindfold of fear to truly embrace it and look forward to your next adventure. Life can be anything you want to make of it based on your internal self-perception, which is governed by your internal emotional state.

Your life experience can become a living nightmare if you continue revolving your life around the illusion of external, man-made, materialistic possessions, mistaking this for what it means to be rich. But being truly rich means having a balanced, emotionally independent state, no longer governed by fear but embracing life with fearlessness and steadfast belief that whatever happens serves your well-being. When things don't go your way, they come with life lessons showing where you need to grow emotionally.

Ultimately, it's about perspective based on your emotional state. That's how you'll experience life regardless of situations—positive or negative. Even in negative circumstances, you'll always see the bright side and handle challenges with compassion, love, and care.

Your past doesn't define who you are. The emotional scars reminding you of pain, joy, love, hate, laughter serve as reminders of your life journey. The past no longer exists. Why carry baggage of feelings that serve no good purpose? Why not learn lessons by recognizing the role we played in our own suffering instead of granting someone else power to dictate how we feel?

The canvas of love is colourful and limitless, filled with joy, love, and abundance. Why not paint the rest of our lives in colours that make your inner child feel alive through authentic living? Pretending to play roles that fit this dysfunctional dogmatic society has served us poorly—why continue? Always remember you have the choice to change your inner reality by connecting with yourself and prioritising your emotional needs.

No one owes us anything, nor do we as adults; everyone will prioritize their emotional needs first—so what stops you? If they're in survival mode due to their emotionally unhealed state and act inconsiderately, you always have the gift of observation to respond and distance yourself. You should never accuse them; they knew what they were doing, yet they acted anyway. For those living in survival mode, the world revolves around them, and they'll continue acting selfishly based on fears as they choose not to heal. Lack of self-awareness, societal conditioning, and disconnection from authentic selves won't instantly transform their apathy into empathy.

Learn to be the bigger person. For your peace of mind, release attachments to emotionally unhealed individuals, relations, family, or friends who remain inconsiderate by choosing not to heal.

To see human beings for who they truly are, observe their character based on human value systems—love, care, empathy, kindness, forgiveness, authenticity, selflessness—not driven by ego based on dogmatic societal structures or man-made constructs. Just as tree bark develops lines with age, our character enhances as we grow. Anything external will never change true human character regardless of adversities faced, because it's based on human moral values and remains unswayed by external influences.

However, narcissists lack character based on human values or internal moral compasses. They see people as objects for emotional dependency, to fulfil their needs, so their personalities change like weather, shapeshifting into different characters according to life situations they encounter. Their character is never based on enduring human values but on materialistic dogmatic imagery creation based on external validation.

Self-sacrificial behaviour that prioritizes others' emotional needs over one's own is self-abandonment. Mostly, women in patriarchal societies are forced to play martyr roles, suffering most by not choosing authentic selves, especially post-marriage. They feel the void and pain daily, continuing to self-sabotage by emotionally investing in their children's lives whilst trying to find existence and meaning in their own.

Women born before the Industrial Revolution in patriarchal societies had no choice in such decisions. But if today's women, who have had proper education and work opportunities, still choose to continue their mothers' generational trauma by being emotionally, financially, and mentally dependent on spouses, then they become part of the problem, alongside caregivers who see them as nothing more than responsibilities and someone else's possessions in this dogmatic society.

First, we must understand that all of us remain somewhat narcissistic as long as we seek external validation to be liked, accepted, and validated, creating individual identities based on dogmatic societal structures and our position according to the same script followed globally. That part reflects vanity and surface-level priorities based on purchasing power within dogmatic societal structures—being accepted and validated for external worth based on money, career, family, children, marriage, relationship status, nationality, purchasing power, home, car, brands, wealth display, etc.

Anything making you abandon your authentic self reflects narcissistic behaviour based on external validation for societal acceptance and status. This feeds our ego based on fears of abandonment, lack of self-worth, fear of rejection, lack of self-acceptance, etc. Until we continue showcasing purchasing power as individual self-expression by attaching identities to nations, cultures, beliefs, brands, cars, families, dogmatic societal structures, homes, luxury trips, idol worship of celebrity culture, entertainment, religion, and spiritual cults, we will continue suffering emotionally and never feel fulfilled as human beings.

Our ego provides only short-term gratification but never allows full healing and acknowledgement of pain that needs addressing, feeling, and recognition as adults by taking accountability and responsibility for our emotional well-being. We need to completely detach emotional worth from these things and realign with authentic selves by choosing to prioritize emotional needs and developing healthy relationships with our inner child.

It might be an isolating journey, but once you understand the power of solitude and your own company, you'll achieve freedom of mind. Once free from anything no longer serving you, you slowly begin loving yourself without comparison, filled with compassion, love, trust, and acceptance. Remember, Rome wasn't built in a day. Creating a relationship with yourself requires reconnecting with your inner child by doing things you loved as a child—singing, painting, writing, dancing, farming, cooking, knitting, drawing, and similar activities—to find outlets for self-expression.

We abandoned such activities because we were constantly compared in school, with families and friends, to determine who was "better." When interacting with someone, focus on feelings you experience—your body signalling through emotions whether you feel safe or unsafe with that person. If you feel safe, you can be authentic with them as they form no judgements. If your body constantly feels unsafe, you tend to argue, become angry, or react to what they say. That person is merely a trigger scratching the surface of the emotional wounds you carry.

Anger tells us we feel disrespected, whilst hate reflects internal wounds from the past that we need to release. We haven't yet accepted all parts of ourselves. Criticism is a byproduct of hate appearing as our inner voice that we need to change through compassion, love, and acceptance. The need for perfection signals narcissistic tendencies and continued self-abandonment by fulfilling emotional needs through external validation from others and man-made societal structures we've based our identity upon, instead of identifying with human values as our true identity.

Our worth is determined by our capacity for love, kindness, generosity, selflessness, empathy, compassion, loyalty, and so forth.

Regarding faith, how we worship and connect with our god matters. Are we practising gratitude for what we have, or asking god to fix problems in our lives? This reflects what kind of person we are. Our relationship with our god turns bitter when we don't receive what we requested, yet we never reflect on why we felt incompetent to solve problems independently. What emotional needs do we have that we cannot provide ourselves, or are these man-made constructs?

When you practise gratitude and speak the heart's language, you'll realize contentment as a person; your relationship with god becomes pure bliss. That's how the universe functions—when you feel blessed, you attract more blessings. We attract what we are. Next time you pray, observe how you speak to yourself and god; it reflects where you stand in your emotional journey and personal growth path. It also reveals self-perception; that's why the world reflected back appears as it does, because you were always responsible for fulfilling emotional needs by taking accountability and responsibility for yourself. Your parents were responsible only until childhood and early teens.

If you dislike what's reflected back, only you hold the key to contentment and happiness—unlock it. See yourself as the powerful force you are, not what the world tells you about yourself. Our inner world creates our outer world, not vice versa. Now you know how to unlock your full potential and understand that becoming your best version lies in how you feel about yourself, not how others make you feel. You control what you allow; no one can touch, manipulate, or control your emotions without your permission. You are and always have been the key to your contentment and happily ever after.

We abandoned our authentic selves long ago, creating likeable personas that are emotionally needed and preferred by others because we continuously self-sacrifice our emotional needs and authentic selves to fit in. This persona is ego-driven, created to meet all the dogmatic societal checklists and benchmarks of the constructed idea of a successful human being. The need for belonging that creates false emotional safety has led us to develop borrowed personalities. Depending on whom we're with, we present sides of ourselves to remain preferred, needed, and relied upon.

We must understand that they like us for the parts of us they've accepted, but they don't love us because they don't know our authentic selves. To evolve, we must abandon the need to be liked and understand that people who provide us emotional safety and see us for who we really are will always love us regardless, because they accept all parts of us. These are the people who contribute to emotional growth and genuinely care about our well-being.

Others attach to us whilst we fulfil their emotional needs and disperse us once satisfied, no longer needing us. That's why friendships formed over self-destructive behaviours like smoking, drinking, or synthetic drugs dissolve when one person no longer needs such coping mechanisms for emotional regulation—the bond disappears because it was based on temporary escapism.

However, bonds formed through emotional understanding and safe spaces where we are authentic and loved will always grow over time, because they're based on mutual respect, consideration, love, and acceptance.

Chapter 8
Love for Vanity

Today's society is structured around vanity, to feel good from the inside. We all want attractive bodies, homes, phones, cars, clothes, food, drinks, brands, and so forth—all revolving around our purchasing power. We inject harmful chemicals into our bodies to look good; we consume chemically synthesized products to build muscle, yet we have no idea about the chemicals used in all the products we consume, inhale, use, eat, and live with. We will do anything today to feel good from the outside, but we have stopped considering the inside. We have accepted that this is how we think, function, and feel. We never question why we are not growing beyond this phase.

Life today is divided into three broad categories: education, work, and retirement. Everyone is jumping through hoops to follow the same model across the globe, with purchasing power determining a person's growth in life. Some want to own homes or cars and eventually marry off the children they have produced. This is how the circle of life is completed today, and literally no one questions who made these rules and why everyone follows them so blindly whilst struggling with them. Meanwhile, milestones are celebrated—degrees, university, relationships, marriage, careers, homes, children, cars, brands owned, travel bucket lists, and retirement. No one sits and questions, "Wait, why are we not asking what my purpose in life is?"

People are busy running like hamsters, showing off what they have achieved in a race by plastering it on social media for external validation. Entertainment, news, politics, celebrity worship, music, sports, cinema, shows, social media, AI, religion, caste, spiritual cults, culture, friends, pets, family, and the accompanying drama fill up the entire human experience for everyone on earth. We are simply living to achieve and fulfil Maslow's hierarchy of needs, mindlessly trying to reach the top to gain societal approval and have a voice that is followed and heard. It's like rushing to be at the top of the food chain to be noticed and worshipped by the rest to feel superior.

No one goes to school to learn what makes them feel alive; they go to school to learn a predetermined curriculum. The same applies to university based on their interests, then getting a career or building a business along those lines. Who decides this is what you can learn from? Why are we not focusing on developing multiple skill sets that interest us? The fear of the unknown from our parents and following the herd puts all of us in schools where we are graded, and due to that, we enter survival mode, trying to fit in, be liked, and get good grades to be loved and accepted. We learn to self-abandon ourselves early in life by not being provided the safe space to decide for ourselves and discover our interests.

No one is bothered to do so; we are rotting with unhealed emotions from our unregulated nervous systems as humans and functioning just like the bright, shiny, genetically modified red tomato that is so appealing to our eyes but tastes nothing like the natural tomato. That is how disconnected we have become as a society from our own humanity because our perception of self and the world is based on beliefs created by a faulty belief system designed to fail us as humans first.

Chapter 9
Discovering Your Self-Worth

We humans have the same emotions as the colour theory of the rainbow. Just as the frequency and wavelength of each colour varies, our thoughts, which are dominated by those emotions in proportion to our time instead of light, govern our internal state and reflect the same back to the external world. The high-frequency emotions that dominate us most in terms of human emotions are fear, anger, and loneliness, which we spend the most time emitting, across the planet. Be it fear of abandonment, not being good enough, fear of rejection, anger over hurt, anger over disrespect, loneliness because of our own sufferings, loneliness in our own company, and so forth.

I would place anticipation in the middle as it can evoke both positive and negative emotions, given the meaning we attach to it. If we are attached to an outcome, we are trying to control things, people, and actions that surround us so we feel emotionally safe, or it can be simply going with the flow and anticipating life as it comes, taking one day at a time—depending on our internal emotional state. Then we encounter human emotions of joy, trust, and peace in our day-to-day lives.

Depending on how healed we are and our emotional state, these emotions are reflected back in our daily life as our thoughts, actions, and behaviour. The more emotionally evolved we are, the more time we spend experiencing joy, trust, and peace as our internal state slowly changes and becomes healthier. We slowly tend to have a positive outlook towards life and everything that surrounds us, once we feel emotionally safe within ourselves by being the best version of our authentic selves.

This doesn't mean we won't experience the remaining emotions; we as humans have a spectrum of emotions, and that's the best part of being human: having the ability to experience all of them. However, with an emotionally healthy state, our perspective, actions, and behaviour with other emotions would be through response rather than reaction. It would be firm but not commanding, and we will continue to fluctuate between these myriad emotions, but we will know how to navigate our emotional waters no matter what uncharted territory we enter in terms of whatever life throws at us, as we have taken accountability and responsibility by being the captain of our own life with our authenticity.

Whenever someone affects our internal emotional state through their actions, words, or behaviour, and if we experience a negative emotional state because of it, we must first be self-aware to understand that we are triggered. Triggers are our biggest blessings and teachers, telling us that this is the part of us that is emotionally wounded and needs to be attended to by us. If we are in a situation where someone causes us to feel disrespected, unworthy, rejected, ashamed, hated, or any other emotion along those lines, we need to understand that people are just different faces playing their part in your life to teach you self-confidence, self-respect, self-love, self-worth, self-trust, authenticity, and self-acceptance.

One will keep encountering the same lessons through different people until we understand that they are all teaching us to stand up for ourselves and work on these unhealed wounds so we stop entertaining people who make us feel emotionally drained instead of safe, cared for, and loved. All we ever needed was validation from ourselves by trusting ourselves and believing in our own abilities, which people might or might not appreciate. We need to stop giving them more power over us to decide the course of our lives.

You are enough and have always been sufficient to know what is best for you. You are the best person to decide what works for you and what doesn't work for you in the first place, as you always have your best interests at heart, as an adult. Sometimes people mean well, but they will always tell you things based on their experience, and most of us have a fear of the unknown and will always give advice and suggestions, sticking to what is tried and tested in this world as safe, no matter what the decision is about. Be it our choice of education, a company we work for, a business we should do, whom we should marry, the location we should live in, whom we should connect with, the friends we make, and so forth.

No one has been in your shoes or had life experiences on your behalf. So giving them power over you will always be detrimental, and you might feel hurt, dejected, and doubtful over your own decisions when they do not react or respond the way you would have wanted them to. Understand that if they are caught up in needing external validation all their lives, how can they agree with authenticity and healing when they are not even self-aware? They don't even realize they have always been seeking external validation to feel emotionally safe in this dogmatic societal structure in the first place. If they have accepted the role assigned by society to play and attached their identity to it, they would never be willing to change the reality they are comfortable with and have attached all their emotions to it by making their existence all about it.

Our human values build our character, and they will always reflect back through the actions we take in our day-to-day lives. We all love someone who is lovable, trustworthy, reliable, selfless, giving, caring, loyal, helpful, empathetic, kind, and so forth. However, many people continue to self-abandon themselves by seeking external validation for these traits from family, friends, relatives, and communities that surround them. We fail to realize that these values must be reflected in our internal state first, and we must develop the ability to give them to ourselves unconditionally. Only then can we be emotionally available for others as human beings in the first place. Otherwise, it is simply a co-dependency situation where people have shared values to fulfil each other's emotional needs and is solely based on attachment. Attachment only leads to conditional love as it is based on emotional dependency, not unconditional love based on emotional independence and the authentic self of multiple individuals.

As Shakespeare said, all the world is a stage, and we are mere actors. We need to shed the role we are born to play without choice in this man-made dogmatic societal structure based on a plan for every individual but not based on purpose for every individual to follow their own path of authenticity by having that emotionally safe space to become emotionally independent in the first place, to learn all the skills they are curious about deciding. Instead, they are entered into a glorified slave mentality early on to either become a ruler or a glorified servant where lives and life plans revolve around money instead of an individual's time, which is their most prized possession on earth as human beings. They are never given a choice to develop the necessary skill set to have the luxury of how they want to spend their time by having that emotionally safe space to create and become their most authentic selves.

Not everyone is equipped to play the part they have been assigned, and hence, as humans, we should have a choice to choose with whom we connect most regarding human values. We might be more nurturing than our mother and more protective than our father. The blame game, as adults, happens when they do not play their designated roles diligently with unconditional love by taking emotional responsibility for the child with an emotionally safe space where they can grow to be their authentic selves with secure attachment. Clearly, this system of dogmatic societal structure is not working, as we all would have made it in life, achieved it all in life, and no more suffering would exist on the planet. We have always had and will always have a choice to build a community based on human values where everyone feels emotionally safe to be their authentic selves, and their authenticity is always encouraged.

If we choose today to shun the role we were given no option to play in this dogmatic society, we give ourselves a chance to develop our authentic character that is emotionally independent and can think what is best for us based on our emotional needs and purpose in life. The character assigned to you according to your family, nation, religion, society, gender, purchasing power, societal structure, and community you are born into is a psychological barrier you have been conditioned to believe as your truth and reality of life as humans. The above-mentioned things have never defined a person's character, so why do we still believe it to be life's truth?

The human mind is complex. Society imposes limitations, making us feel trapped in toxic work cultures. This leads to envy of those with wealth. We often equate money with freedom and neglect our dreams due to fear of the unknown. This mindset keeps us in a cycle of self-imposed limitations.

The elite benefit from our acceptance of this system, where we work hard for future security whilst struggling with mental health issues. We use distractions—such as alcohol and social media—to avoid confronting ourselves. As we chase wealth, we become obsessed with status, forgetting what truly matters—human connection and doing what we love. The illusion created by society pressures us to conform, often at the cost of our well-being.

We are fed toxic products marketed by celebrities who do not have our best interests at heart. Brands prioritize profit over health, contributing to a cycle of consumption and waste. The entertainment industry profits from our desire for escape, whilst many brands exploit child labour and environmental resources. We continue to support these practices, neglecting the harm they cause.

To break free, we must reclaim our power, prioritize authenticity, and focus on what brings us joy. We can build a healthier community by supporting those caring for others. Ultimately, our worth isn't defined by wealth or status. We must resist the urge to conform to societal pressures and strive for a life rooted in compassion and purpose.

All these are man-made things, and if they no longer serve you, you have full right to exercise your free will to choose what is best for your authentic self to move towards peace, joy, and trust. You do not have to keep suffering due to a man-made dogmatic societal structure that has been made to control and keep you in survival mode so that you as an individual will never think about yourself and the structure that keeps you enslaved. Our character as humans has and always will be defined by who we are from the inside, not by being someone's son, daughter, brother, sister, mother, father, and so forth. It is based on the human values of our ability to be loving, kind, generous, selfless, empathetic, sensitive, compassionate, loyal, authentic, honest, trustworthy, helpful, and so forth. The more we focus on healing our internal state by seeing ourselves based on human values instead of seeking anything external to express our individuality, the more we will evolve and grow emotionally with time. Money is and always will be a byproduct, and it has nothing to do with human emotions, values, or needs.

Our only limitation is our mind; human potential is infinite. We often tie our individuality to external brands rather than focusing on internal growth. Emotional growth is essential. We must replace the love of money with self-love. Chasing what others have brings only temporary satisfaction, leading to a cycle of distraction and superficial gratification. Instead, we should work on nurturing our inner fulfilment.

It is when our hearts are open and genuinely listening to our emotions and authentic selves that it can navigate us, through intuition, as our navigation towards living the best version of life. Those benefiting from this imbalance of inequality created by this dogmatic societal structure—money hoarders, patriarchy, religion, public figures, entertainers, brand owners, and so forth—will never change because they will lose the audience of individuals with slave-mentalities who were always leaders of their own lives in the first place. All these beliefs only made them give their power away and tie themselves to an imaginary leash, to be led by those due to these self-created psychological barriers, due to the conditioning of the mind through the cultural, social, economic, societal, national, political, religious, spiritual and cults and family belief systems.

Our worth correlates to other people's emotional investment towards us as a brand. For example, the sale of music records, concert ticket prices, news, PR, and investment in such celebrities' personal life news puts them up the hierarchy and makes them role models of the life everyone aspires to have. Their image is sold as someone who has it all together, a path to unlimited money and happiness like a genie with unlimited wishes. No one questions the carbon emissions the elite are causing and contributing to global warming by exploiting such man-made privileges, nor is anyone asking why they are not giving back at least 50% of their wealth to society despite seeing the rise in poverty across the globe, as they are financially secure for generations to come.

Other people's actions towards you always reflect their own perception of self and the world. We should never take it personally. It is and has never been about us. If you have ever been cheated on, disrespected, and not valued as a person, it is because that is how the other person sees themselves. It will always reflect back in their behaviour towards others, be it their partner, family, or friends. People's inability to stay loyal, jumping from relationship to relationship, being abusive, disrespectful, inconsiderate, selfish, and lying and cheating, is a direct reflection of their inner world. Imagine being surrounded by these values 24/7 via your own thoughts. These people are tormented enough by their own misery; the best thing one can do is disassociate from such people and just be glad that they are no longer suffering because of someone's inability to heal themselves.

Currently, everyone you see is still reliving their childhood wounds as adults, given knowingly and unknowingly by caregivers, family, entertainment, dogmatic societal systems, and the schooling system based on conditional love—be it issues with self-worth, self-trust, fear of abandonment, fear of rejection, self-hatred, self-sabotage, and so forth. So we avoid being with ourselves, and the entertainment industry, influencers, money, careers, schools, university, brands, nations, politics, religious groups, spiritual groups, society, family setups, spouses, relationships, hookups, flings, relatives, and friends continue to promote our emotional co-dependency by giving us a false sense of emotional safety and belonging. In reality, it doesn't help us become emotionally independent by never allowing us an emotionally safe environment to think for ourselves. It always promotes groupthink behaviour and discourages anyone who thinks for themselves by keeping their emotions first as selfish and self-centred.

We also need to understand that when we live in survival mode, we make decisions based on our coping mechanisms to feel good from the inside by being dependent on external factors to give us dopamine, oxytocin, and serotonin—be it people, alcohol, hookups, flings, gambling, eating unhealthy food, shopping, trips, and so forth. There is a desperate need to fit in and show it off on social media and to people, as we have based our identities on it by attaching our emotions to external factors. We need them to feel emotionally safe and cope without realizing that we need to feel secure emotionally in our bodies.

The only way we can do that is to acknowledge these emotional wounds we carry, which have led to destructive coping mechanisms for us as adults because we always think we need others. The need to fit into setups based on belief systems like family, relationship, friendship groups, religion, caste, creed, nation, politics, entertainment, Maslow's hierarchy of money-based needs, purchasing power to buy brands, social media followers, lifestyle, food choices, and so forth is based on a man-made system. It is not aligned with our human values or our internal emotional safety in the first place.

Don't get me wrong; it's in our DNA, and we need to belong, but it is the opposite of fitting in. When someone gives you an emotionally safe space to share your feelings without judgement or preconceived notions, accepts you the way you are in your most authentic self, and helps you grow emotionally as a human being, those are the ones with whom we should build our community of belonging.

Often, most of us have an inherent need to be liked and feel a sense of belonging that we attach to safety; the need stems from our childhood to be liked by our caregivers, teachers, and friends at school, which constitutes our external environment. But in being popular, needed, and wanted, we end up with a false persona altered by people-pleasing tendencies. We give our sense of worth to others and constantly dress, talk, and do things to fit in and be well-liked. Often, we try to put others' needs above our own by self-sacrificing our own, and we end up abandoning our authenticity in the process.

When we are not the child the teacher or classmates or our caregiver gives their undivided attention to, the message we get is that something must be wrong with us, due to which they prefer someone else over us. The top scorer is glorified, and their grades are put up there for everyone to see with the teacher gushing over them. It sends a message to a child that someone else is better than them, and they have to earn love by proving their worth through grades. So a child enters the slave mentality of slogging away by not being a child but staying trapped at a study table trying to learn something they are not interested in just to get the desired grades to prove they are lovable—again, a classic case of self-abandonment by not choosing their authentic interests and being themselves, which was enough for them to be liked. It puts us in a box we never leave until we retire, but by then, we are too old to the extent that we can barely do things we wanted and end up regretting the life we lived by not doing things we wanted to do.

Imagine being a primitive hunter who has gone out in the forest to gather food, but the hunter is always on their toes trying to save themselves from wild animals. The fight-and-flight response is active in the body, and they are scared to make a single mistake due to the fear of being attacked or killed. So if a tiger gets in the way, the hunter kills it to survive; if a goat crosses the path, the hunter kills it for food. In both instances, the hunter has taken a life without the animal's consent because it was focused on its survival.

You will agree with the story and everything the hunter did because it makes sense. The decisions were based on survival instincts that go against the human values of empathy, kindness, compassion, love, forgiveness, care, and selflessness. The hunter was in survival mode, so it was selfish, self-centred, unkind, unjust, and lacked compassion, empathy, carefulness, and showed cruelty. They acted inhumanely, which, in normal circumstances, if they had an unlimited supply of food on their table, they wouldn't do. Let's not take this analogy to justify the killing of innocent lives, be it humans or animals, but to understand the psychology behind it.

If a nicely dressed human on the outside has the same fearful mindset as the hunter, they will do the same thing to other humans; they will hurt you, be inconsiderate, will not care about your emotions, will lack compassion, lack kindness, will be selfish, unempathetic, and downright cruel to you. We need not take the actions of others in today's world personally. It is not about us; it is their life where they are in this hunter's survival mindset. So the choices, behaviour, and actions will not be based on human values of love, kindness, compassion, consideration, empathy, loyalty, or selflessness. Instead, they would be based on all the survival-based belief systems based on money, and we are running like hamsters in a wheel with no direction, trying to hoard cash to survive.

If we feel emotionally hurt by such individuals, we understand the burden they feel due to their own self-created suffering of negative thoughts in their minds every day. The best thing to do whilst dealing with such individuals, if we cannot offer them compassion due to our self-respect, is to let go of them with grace; their mind is a mental prison for them already. Holding on to resentment over someone already punishing themselves every day with their own thoughts by constantly being in survival mode and going against the human value system by always acting based on a man-made internal limiting belief system is a punishment in itself.

Always remember, anyone can only give you what they have. If they are not emotionally available for themselves first by being in a state of constant survival, expecting them to be there for you is on us. Holding on to resentment over such individuals, be it our caregivers, friends, family, colleagues, or partners, will add to our misery. We cannot change what happened to us in our past, and by holding on to it, we are just adding to our misery by making it about us. The choices and actions people take are on them. It is never about us; it is always a reflection of their internal emotional state that reflects back to everyone they interact with.

The wise thing here is to learn grace and lessons to grow emotionally and move on from it. Sometimes, no closure is the closure we need to understand our lessons. Navigate your life forward with grace and let go of the resentment towards others who have wronged you in the past or present.

Chapter 10
The Art of Letting Go

Our perception of ourselves and the world around us determines how we live our lives. Our internal state reflects back on how we see others. However, often when we expect them to keep us emotionally safe as adults, it causes conflict. Usually, we do not leave the situation because we are attached to an outcome and are not present in the situation as it exists. For example, we date multiple potential partners and keep going with the flow without arriving at a destination. In reality, we are not emotionally ready to take responsibility for anyone else because we are too scared to be hurt or vulnerable again. We fear heartbreak, and the mind often reminds us of past instances of how much it took from us.

So we suppress our authentic selves and real emotions and do not voice our expectations to others. Often we do, and when they are not ready, we are the ones who get hurt. If, heaven forbid, they choose someone else over us, we end up blaming them for the feelings of unworthiness we experience. We fail to realize that we are the ones who allowed ourselves to enter a situation where we did not feel emotionally safe due to other people's actions. Still, we had an external need—fear of being alone—and we were seeking love, so we chose to stay in situations where we felt mistreated, disrespected, insecure, and unworthy. We stayed because we saw ourselves through those emotions due to our childhood emotional wounds.

We tried to control the outcome and their behaviour to align with what we wanted from the situation, continuously ignoring the red flags and our emotions. With time, we often lose respect, love, and feelings of emotional safety with such people. Still, due to our attachment and fear of abandonment, we keep holding on to such relationships that are not emotionally fulfilling by reliving the same childhood reality of being unloved again and again.

Always remember that the choices of other individuals are based on their narrative and perception of themselves and the world around them. How they feel about themselves is how they will act and be attracted to the outside world. Conflict of the mind is directly proportional to the conflicts we face in our realities. So if you meet someone who cannot seem to stay alone and keeps jumping from relationship to relationship, it is not because they are searching for love; it is because they like being needed and are heavily dependent on others to feel good from the inside.

All the choices anyone makes are based on fulfilling their emotional needs; sometimes these choices are self-destructive, and sometimes they are based on fears. These needs are solely based on emotional wounds from childhood that we have not healed by releasing the trauma, beliefs, and self-perception attached to them. What others do has nothing to do with us; we never need anyone more than we need our own authentic self to show up for us, every time, in all the situations life throws at us.

Remember, if the actions of others hurt you, it comes from expectations and your own perception of self regarding what you would have done in a situation like that. But you are not them, so you cannot understand the struggles of their mind based on the emotional wounds they still carry inside. What we can do is what is best for us whilst simultaneously giving such people grace even when their actions hurt us, because it was never about us. Let it go and free ourselves from any attachment that no longer serves you and does not add to your emotional growth regarding how you perceive yourself and the world around you.

Understand that the other person does not see the world through your eyes because you are not in the same place regarding emotional growth. They do not belong in the reality you have created by overcoming your struggles and working through your emotional wounds and healing. The more you delay the inevitable, the more you will allow yourself to suffer by abandoning your authenticity and shrinking your existence to match someone else's world.

We do this because of our psychological belief in a false sense of belongingness and emotional safety based on attachment and emotional dependency on others, revolving around our identities based on society, family, friendships, nation, customs, religion, relationships, and groupthink behaviour. They are all tuned to the same frequency of unhealed emotional wounds we seek to heal. It is familiar to the nervous system as it knows how to navigate its way around both the internal (emotional) environment and external (people) environment around us.

We know how to navigate around individuals with such unhealed, emotionally unregulated nervous systems because we depend emotionally on each other for secure attachments based on emotional co-dependency. The constant exposure to this acts as a building block of trauma bonding over shared beliefs, issues, customs, religion, thoughts, coping mechanisms, codependent attachments, and so forth.

There is no authenticity in such a setup where one can carve one's identity based on self-discovery, life experiences, and learning by having that emotionally safe space to grow authentically. Consider such setups as a group project of emotional growth where everyone is drawing the same house, stuck in the same class for generations, displaying groupthink behaviour, and having the same conflicts of not feeling emotionally fulfilled and safe with each other. Still, they keep choosing to collaborate as adults because of the heavy emotional dependency on each other to feel safe based on the false construct of the man-made family system, as they have never been provided with an emotionally safe environment as children to be authentic, emotionally independent, emotionally regulated to create a healthy nervous system, and to be genuine. Such people permanently live in survival mode and give more importance to what others think about them rather than what they feel from the inside about these other people.

People will only change when they want to make a difference. No matter how much we tell them we want them to be part of our life's journey because of our emotional dependency and attachment towards them to feel emotionally safe and secure, what we are trying to do is avoid being hurt, so we keep telling them to mould themselves to make us feel emotionally safe. This is what plays out in many relationship dynamics today. But instead of questioning what we lack emotionally to be dependent on them in the first place, we tend to blame them for their choices that hurt us. It comes from expecting them to act whilst keeping our emotions in mind.

However, we need to realize that if someone is living in survival mode, the last thing they would have is consideration towards others because emotionally they are not in a place where they are even considerate towards themselves. Even if we cannot relate to the choices they made or if their choices hurt us, we need to realize that they were trying to survive in their self-created reality of suffering from their own mind and thoughts that they have carried from childhood to adulthood. They made these choices due to a lack of awareness of these emotional wounds and attachment patterns and were doing whatever it took to soothe themselves or cope, even if it was destructive.

Compassion should not be limited to self, and neither should forgiveness. The only power we have is to teach ourselves to give people grace. The environment they are born into is not by choice; they were never provided with the right tools to cope. So they learn unhealthy coping mechanisms as children to deal with it. However, they keep repeating these coping mechanisms as adults, that are destructive, to feel good about themselves when their external environment was always unsafe in childhood.

The anger and resentment they carry towards their caregiver is valid because anger is your friend who, as an emotion, tells you when you are being disrespected and mistreated. But we must understand that it is for the wounds we carry from childhood and towards our caregivers. The only way to get justice for those mistreatments—where we had to abandon our authenticity to choose unhealthy attachment to our caregiver to live with their conditional love and belief system—is by understanding that they are the only ones accountable for it. Taking it out on others is not fair to them in adulthood, be it our friends, partners, or relatives.

As adults, we can remove ourselves from environments or people that no longer make us feel emotionally safe. Building that trust with love and compassion within ourselves from within is how we heal such wounds, and the anger dissipates with time. We slowly learn to trust that we will never allow anyone to have access to us emotionally if they are not emotionally safe for us by setting firm boundaries and taking our time to get to know people.

First, we need to feel emotionally safe and secure within by fulfilling all the emotional needs that we sought in our caregiver that were unfulfilled and for which we are still emotionally dependent on others to fulfil—in terms of external validation to feel confident, secure, worthy, lovable, respected, and accepted as humans.

We need to understand that the world does not revolve around us. The need to control everyone around us and know everything comes from feeling emotionally unsafe, as we are attached and dependent on others. Families and relatives see you as a group instead of an individual, and they feel a sense of entitlement over one's individual life. Their focus is to mould one into their own thinking, beliefs, and customs without providing them with a choice to think for themself.

Since childhood, one attaches one's identities to such beliefs, customs, and groupthink behaviour due to emotional dependency and a false sense of belongingness in the family structure. Parents parade their children around as a false sense of milestones, like a prized possession, flaunting their grades, university, careers, purchasing power, marriage, and children. They need to externally validate themselves in front of the false sense of community they have built with family and relatives to gain their approval. They spend so much money just to feed people and see their children married that it becomes like a lifelong dream for them to find partners for their kids or celebrate such milestones.

Emotional independence is never considered a parenting job because it is the opposite of what a family unit should be, as the choice to choose a family is something a child never has in a dogmatic society. You are born into a family, and even if it is unhealthy for your emotional health, you are forced to be part of such a structure. People have children to complete their family due to heavy conditioning. Hence, conditional love comes in as they see the child as an extension of themselves and want them to carry forward their family name.

However, if we are emotionally invested in someone and they do not make us feel emotionally secure over time, it is only up to us to walk out of such situations. We need to remember that as adults, we have a choice to move out of such equations; we are no longer living in survival mode the way we did in our childhood because we were emotionally, mentally, and financially dependent on our caregivers to look after us as they procreated us. We were born into such families with no consent as babies.

As adults, we need to understand that we no longer live in the same environment and are trying to gain approval or validation from our caregivers to feel emotionally secure. We are responsible for ourselves, and we need to choose ourselves first. If we keep choosing people who do not make us feel emotionally safe, we are again abandoning ourselves. Then we end up neglecting our needs and feelings, feeling ashamed, disrespected, and unworthy of our love for self as we choose attachment over authenticity.

Remember, we do not need anyone to feel emotionally secure as adults; all we ever needed was to heal ourselves and feel safe from within. The need to depend on others comes from unhealed emotional wounds that need soothing. Often, we choose destructive patterns of behaviour such as meaningless sex, jumping from relationship to relationship due to our inability to stay alone, and dissociative behaviour of binge eating, drinking, watching, smoking, and so forth.

The fear of loneliness is the reason more than half the world is married today, justifying the right age to marry as a parameter for finding someone, or people are busy in different types of complex relationship patterns to fulfil their emotional needs to feel the thrill of the chase for a surface-level connection. It happens because we are dissociated from our emotions and lack depth and understanding of who we are. So we tend to base our identities on things, people, materialistic endeavours, purchasing power, brands, homes, job titles, car ownership, clothes we wear, and places we can afford to live, visit, and travel as an expression of individual personality—of how we have made it in this world. We do this to seek external validation, but deep down, we cannot even spend an hour alone with our own thoughts and minds today.

Chapter 11

Finding Your Purpose

You cannot have a checklist and plan your life as you have been told. We are not here to get an education, work, marry, have children, and eventually die whilst earning loads of money and becoming money hoarders in the process. This plan makes us hamsters on the wheel of life, mindlessly running with no destination, plan, or purpose. Most humans following the dogmatic societal structure of followers are caught up in this; they see money as the bait and mindlessly chase it whilst having no defined purpose towards their existence.

There is no timestamp to the experiences that come into your life. The need to control things to feel safe makes us plan our future. What makes us so worried about our near future if we do not know what will happen to us in the next five minutes? We have these bizarre goals according to societal standards and deem them happiness. We are so attached to the idea of finally being happy and getting our happily ever after that all we can see is achieving that goal no matter what. We keep jumping from relationship to relationship every year or so. We never realize the pattern we follow when we seek someone first; we are searching for love when we are always supposed to find it within ourselves first. We seek what we do not have to feel complete.

If we do not love ourselves unconditionally as adults, it is no one's job but ours as adults to do so. We see the world through our perception of self and create our reality around it as that is our radio frequency, and we keep connecting to the channels in the form of people who do not love themselves either. Depending on your emotional growth stage, your radio frequency keeps changing, and you keep tuning into the channels operating on the same frequency.

The moment you realize that all you need to do is find love within yourself by being the best version of your authentic real self, you understand you only sought it because you were running away from your authentic self and you kept abandoning yourself to escape the suppressed emotions you had not yet dealt with from childhood. The only way out is to feel all the emotional range that resides in us, which is stored in our body as trauma, and our hearts keep reminding us to feel it to heal it.

Imagine yourself as Mario. Every level you clear is based on emotional growth by learning lessons from people. So at every level, the same people cannot be the obstacles and blessings in your journey. Not everyone will believe in evolving or working on themselves. Letting go of people who no longer serve you or add to your emotional growth, so you can move ahead in life, is something you need to do if you want to evolve emotionally as a human being. It is your responsibility as an adult to take accountability for your actions and take care of your emotional needs by fulfilling them on your own. This can only be achieved when we strive to become emotionally independent. Until then, even as adults, we will rely on others to care for our emotional needs; we will always depend on someone to validate our emotions externally.

One also needs to understand that we are trying to change years of conditioning and reprogram our minds by choosing to change our current reality with an understanding that our traumas are the facts that the brain puts forward as results whenever we are faced with something new and try to analyse if it is emotionally safe for us or not. The past stories are in the past; we cannot pass judgement on others based on our experiences. We must treat our brains like the news channels today, wired to tell everything wrong in our inner world, whilst the news does the same in our external world, playing with our emotions based on fear of losing our authentic self and emotional safety attached to man-made things and societal constructs.

Our thoughts are different channels; we keep switching between them. We are so stuck on feel-good ones because the rest are fear-inducing that we develop unhealthy coping mechanisms to keep chasing those dopamine receptors to feel good from the inside by ticking off things according to social constructs and dogmatic society to keep our sense of existence alive, valid, and meaningful.

The first method to change our perspective towards our internal and external environment is by being mindful. We need to understand that we no longer have to abandon our authentic selves and choose our attachment patterns, be they anxious, avoidant, or dismissive, as we depended on our caregivers to fulfil our emotional needs. We can be the adults today who can fulfil those needs; we no longer need to follow the same patterns that are still leading us to abandon ourselves and keeping us emotionally suffocated.

So all the thoughts we developed in childhood due to our conditioning of the conscious mind are based on fear and attachments where we had to suppress or hide parts of ourselves to be loved and liked by everyone around us. With this realisation, we can understand that we, as helpless children, were living in survival mode to cope and keep ourselves emotionally safe in an environment where we had no choice but to be around our caregivers, relatives, friends, and in our school or university.

Now, as adults, if we continue living in the same survival mode, despite our external environment having changed and us having the right to exercise free will and live authentically, what happens is we are still trapped due to our psychological and emotional wounds given to us in our childhood. We need to realize that as adults, we are no longer trapped, but our mind still functions with the same thoughts and internal belief systems attached to our childhood identities to survive. So it always runs on a fear-based model, connected to the external environment with the belief that you must live in a dogmatic societal structure based on money to be happy.

Happiness is and always will be internal; the state of joy is felt from the inside, and the only way to master it is by completely detaching yourself from any attachments you have to others by becoming emotionally independent so you can love people for who they are, not because you are societally tagged to them.

Our thoughts can either make us or keep us in survival mode for the rest of our lives. Just as one does a diet cleanse to lose extra pounds here and there, do an environmental cleanse. For the external environment, to avoid living in a dissociative state, limit your screen time and exposure to entertainment, news, and social media to no more than half an hour a day. Only expose yourself to an emotionally healthy environments, be it positive words or daily conversations around you with family, friends, or partners.

Spend time alone with yourself and get back to things that make you feel content, be it reading, journalling, listening to music, writing, singing, dancing, going on walks, or playing sports. This is the way we connect back to our inner child, from childhood, before we passed self-judgement on things we are good and bad at, so we stopped doing things that made our inner child feel alive when someone told us we are bad at drawing, singing, or dancing, and we chose to believe it by comparing ourselves to others.

Remember solving puzzles as children? Just consider your life at the moment as a puzzle. Instead of seeing what went wrong or who wronged you, see what you lacked in terms of self-worth, respect, attachment issues, fear of loneliness, abandonment, and so forth, where we have not put our authenticity first and ended up abandoning ourselves in those situations. Now you will get answers along the lines of, "Oh, I stayed in that relationship for so long but never felt emotionally safe because I had a fear of abandonment and rejection, and low self-esteem."

That is how we put the pieces of our past together; it is no longer the emotional wound we still carry, but it becomes the scar of the soldier in us, that reminds us of the internal battle of the conscious mind based on conditioned beliefs which doubted our own infinite capabilities. We have managed to slay the negative patterns of thinking based on fear and have grown emotionally as people.

The structure and the educational system exist just to enhance the development of your left brain, whereas proper right-brain development is completely ignored and not cared for. We humans need a balanced system to provide both brains with opportunities to develop and evolve in an emotionally safe environment where the child is never pressured mentally so that our sympathetic nervous system is always relaxed in our developmental years. However, comparison in school for grades every year is introduced so that it becomes a core part of the training of glorified slaves, so our body produces and starts dealing with cortisol at a very early age.

Left-brain development is implemented across the globe so that we are always ruled by logic and never develop emotional intelligence based on creativity to arrive at a balanced state of functioning that is in sync with our emotions and logic. We learn to internalize these emotions of shame, unworthiness, insecurity, entitlement, and abandonment at an early age. Then our emotions become emotionally dependent on our peers, who bully us if we do not dress, act, or talk like them or do not score similar marks by mocking our intelligence. The glorification of top scorers by teachers and principals crushes our self-respect and confidence.

If creativity was such a bad thing, why do we seek solace in art, poems, songs, dance, and so forth to deal with our emotions, when we are suffering, as an outlet to connect with our internal emotional state? It always brings us a sense of calmness and peace from the inside. Nature itself is creative in so many ways. Have you looked at the shape of different creations, be they trees, rocks, animals, birds, or amphibians? The colours of the sky, sea, food, trees, and so forth? Listening to the sound of a waterfall, the ocean, a river, rain or birds. Walking in the mountains always makes us feel alive and curious and connects with the innermost part of ourself by giving us a sense of peace. Humans are part of nature, so how can we expect ourselves to act differently according to the dogma of societal structure that keeps us away from our core nature?

We are revolving our lives around increasing our purchasing power and moving to confined, overpopulated cities where we are nothing but glorified slaves who believe they are in control, but we are giving away our precious time—our ticket to life on earth. We have no control over the cost of living, the confined spaces we live in, the food we eat, the water we drink, the air we breathe, and we barely get a few weeks to connect with nature and ourselves.

Yes, we are happily living this lie and showing everyone how successful we are whilst accepting our role as a follower to some corporation with job roles that mostly barely allow us to showcase our creative skills in the first place. Nor do most of us have the option to move to any location across the globe to live on our own terms. We treat our careers just like transactional relationships where we are getting paid for the value we add due to our skill set in exchange for money.

No one is asking why we are forced to come to offices when clearly all of us kept the world running whilst sitting at home during COVID-19. Why force us to return to such expensive cities to spend maximum time in their lifeless offices and commute to prime areas where we can barely afford rent? Why are we still agreeing to this modern-day glamourized slavery where we do not have a choice based on what is convenient for us in the first place?

Our faulty and conditional dogmatic societal belief systems create psychological barriers in our perception towards self and others; they do nothing but divide us and leave us high and dry to deal with all the negative emotions of hatred, jealousy, envy, anger, power, greed, inhumanness, and cruelty based on man-made constructs of dogmatic societal divisions between humankind. These create psychological barriers using money, economy, politics, technology, nations, religion, surnames, caste, customs, culture, food, beverage, education systems based on ranking, celebrities, procreation, governance, influencers, purchasing power, news, media, entertainment, lifestyle, careers, bank balance, and brands.

Only by mastering our negative emotions and dismantling such heavy conditioning by detaching our feelings from it can we construct a safe space by reprogramming our beliefs based on human values to evolve and grow emotionally as humans by developing a healthy nervous system to regulate our emotions internally. All we ever needed was the courage to choose ourselves every time and become emotionally independent as adults so that no one could govern us.

No matter where you are, you should be entirely and irrevocably in love with yourself from within. That means loving all the parts, especially those you were taught to hate first or hide from the rest of the world to fit in and be liked by many. Once you love yourself unconditionally by reprogramming your brain over what individual expression of self actually means versus what we were heavily conditioned by—not associating yourself with any belief system that defines you and puts you in a box—you will stop seeking love externally and let it come to you when the time is right.

The whole concept of finding someone else who completes you is a programme that does not allow us to have a deeper understanding of who we are without any noise or clutter; it keeps us trapped within an old-age concept packaged beautifully as a heavenly feeling—that we need to seek love or be in love to feel alive for the first time in our lives. As adults, we must understand that we chase the feelings we experience when in love, from different faces across time, because we are not taught to give the same feelings to ourselves.

Again, it is an ingrained belief that you need that feeling externally by having someone else, to feel complete about yourself. We only fall for words because they give us a sense of what we lack in terms of emotional security within ourselves; when such an individual's actions do not match their words, our core childhood wound comes to light. The pain you feel is a reminder of what you need to heal internally. Any distractions will only act as a band-aid but will always leave you feeling empty.

Becoming emotionally intelligent requires you to have an open mind where you have to unlearn everything you have ever been taught that keeps you in the box of ego; it requires you to dismantle everything and become a seeker of knowledge, looking for answers every day just as you did when you were a little child. It is a shock to start over and realize that the entire societal structure always sets you up for failure, but being in denial and not having an open mind to reset and live an authentic real life, poses a risk that is is far more significant than that.

Chapter 12
The Power of Love and Self-Respect

Love has always been invaluable and humankind's most significant emotional currency. Unfortunately, we have always been taught to seek it and never taught how to give it to ourselves in the first place. We only seek what we do not know how to provide ourselves with internally—love and positive feelings. We seek love from caregivers, friends, family, and partners because we need it most to feel safe and secure as human beings. Society is structured so that we are always emotionally dependent on others—whether caregivers, friends, family, or spouses—to make us feel good internally.

However, we are never taught that we cannot pour from an empty cup, and we seek love so desperately because we are never taught how to give it to ourselves freely and unconditionally first. To love yourself unconditionally is and has always been an individual journey of self-learning, and we do not need anyone to give it to us until we know how to give it to ourselves freely first. Only then will we develop the capacity to love others freely without any conditions, social norms, or entitlement to be related by law as adults.

The ability to love ourselves unconditionally as humans is our greatest gift and is directly proportional to attaining the highest emotional intelligence, which comes with mastering our negative emotions and reprogramming our belief system that acts as a roadblock to our connection with our innate human values and emotions.

Our unconditional love towards our self enables us to attain the highest form of emotional intelligence that all of us can achieve. Once we do that, we see the bigger picture of what life actually means by removing the glasses of faulty belief systems that separate us from our human values, hinder our emotional growth, and stop us from evolving as humans in the first place.

Evolution is not limited to the capabilities of the mind as a creator with technology that we see today in scientific research; it is actually to move away from survival with an emotionally unhealed, unregulated nervous system towards thriving mode by creating a safe internal environment so that your pituitary gland is no longer regulating cortisol in your body. Your pineal gland produces and regulates serotonin and melatonin in your body so you can elevate and tap into your evolved, unlimited creative potential as an authentic human by having your heart and mind in sync with each other—mastering your negative emotions and thriving to your fullest potential.

The inability to love ourselves unconditionally today is reflecting in failed relationships, family dynamics, and friendships where resentments have taken the front seat. All this is because we trusted our caregivers as children to make us feel emotionally secure. However, due to their own conditional self-love based on societal constructs, they ended up being emotionally unavailable to us in ways we needed to be cared for. We had to abandon ourselves and choose the attachment—be it anxious, avoidant, or dismissive—that our caregiver provided us with their conditional love, as we were emotionally dependent on them to take care of us as children.

We as adults still carry the baggage of unhealed emotional wounds transferred internally by our caregivers in terms of shame, fears, hatred, beliefs, comparison, anger, rage, abandonment, guilt, co-dependency, and unworthiness through their words and actions, with an unhealthy attachment pattern due to these childhood wounds. We as adults learn to conditionally accept only parts of us that were acceptable to our emotionally wounded caregiver by giving up our authenticity and ending up suffering emotionally in the same manner as our caregivers.

We end up being exact replicas of our emotionally unavailable parents, and this reflects in our choices of partners. This is how we end up inheriting generational trauma without realising it, as it all depends on feeling emotionally safe from within. If we continue with the same unhealed, emotionally unregulated system, we will not be able to grow our emotional intelligence as adults. It is vital to have a healthy, regulated nervous system, and that can only be achieved when we take steps towards becoming entirely emotionally independent as human beings.

Our societal structure does not teach us to be emotionally healthy first as adults; instead, it promotes us always seeking relationships for love rather than seeking it inside ourselves first. Such relationships are prevalent today—two unhealed people come together with the same triggers and emotional wounds due to subconscious choice and attraction based on childhood experiences and, in most cases, end up marrying each other due to the intensity of the connection, as they never felt the same way about anyone else.

However, in the long run, such relationships are lifeless, lack respect and love, and they never feel emotionally safe with each other as adults. They end up accusing each other all their lives of not loving them unconditionally, the same way they always felt about their caregiver of the opposite sex. Such adults eventually latch onto their children for love and live through them later in their lives. This is widespread in joint families and arranged marriage setups, as the decision to get married is never based on emotional safety built on human values of a person and, most of the time, is decided by their families based on external factors like looks, money, degree, career, family name, family's bank balance, culture, religion, caste, age, body, and so forth.

With the understanding that the reason we no longer connect with particular individuals after a certain period is due to a lack of emotional connection and self-love, some are still suffering because of their inability to stay alone and unhealthy attachments to toxic people around them. Such people keep jumping from relationship to relationship that only involve surface-level interactions based on dopamine. When things get serious and unhealed wounds we carry from childhood flare up, we go back to seeking someone else to fill the loneliness we feel inside.

It is a toxic loop that ends up making us feel drained, emotionally overwhelmed, and hurt. Until we realize that it is our own unhealthy nervous system based on emotional dysregulation that is responsible for such choices and wounds in the first place—where we are giving strangers full access to how we feel every day by handing them the remote to our emotions because of our external dependency to feel good from inside and our inability to deal with our negative emotions—we will not be able to break this toxic cycle of external emotional co-dependency on others to feel good about ourselves as adults.

To break a cycle like this, one needs to understand that you are not emotionally weak; do not let others tell you otherwise due to lack of self-confidence. Focus on building self-confidence to see your worth even if no one else does. You alone have always been enough; do not let the world make you believe otherwise. As adults, we are equipped enough to change our reality if we do not like the one we are in. We as humans have the power to learn self-regulation of our own emotions, but this will only come when we keep an open mind and no longer follow the herd mentality of those who are still living in survival mode because they do not want to change their reality and would like to continue with the false perception of self that the societal structure has brainwashed them to believe.

It is acceptable to cut ties with people who are not good for your emotional health. It does not matter if they are your immediate family, relatives, spouse, or friends. If they constantly push your buttons and your body does not feel safe in their company, or you feel emotionally drained, you have the full right as an adult to limit their access to your life. This is self-care, not selfishness. Your self-respect should always come first; until you learn how to honour yourself and set your boundaries, your body will always feel traumatized due to the abandonment your emotions feel when you do not listen to how you feel.

The environment around you that encourages you to seek love in others to feel complete sets you up for failure. One must seek wholeness from within and love oneself unconditionally first, to love freely without attachments or expectations from others. Otherwise, we are empty vessels living in self-created chaos whilst looking for others to fulfil our basic needs as adults.

When we depend on someone else to take care of our emotional needs, as taught by the societal programming of what the right way to live is, what we end up doing by following it is holding someone else accountable for not taking care of our emotional needs and making us feel safe, just as we did in childhood with our caregivers. This is majorly reflected in all relationships across the globe today. We hold others accountable for our emotional state, and the other person always feels like they are tiptoeing around us.

The resentment most of us carry in adult bodies by choosing not to heal because justice was never served—we fail to realize that the only power we have within is to learn our lessons and move on. This is the closure; anyone who knowingly or unknowingly did what they did to you as adults knew what they were doing in the first place. The best response is to accept them for who they are and change your environment by making it safe for yourself as an adult to be expressive and secure.

We are never taught to be the best version of ourselves by exploring our individuality; we are also made to think and believe things as a herd (labelled as family belief systems). Our caregivers' belief systems are their biggest psychological weapon used to divide us; they have already been programmed and brainwashed by placing all their worth on this external man-made system and end up teaching us the same life with conditional love and care, as they were also never allowed to express individuality internally and only understood or were dependent on external forces as an expression of individual self in this man-made money-based society.

If our caregiver is not emotionally intelligent, carries unhealed trauma, and does not know how to regulate emotionally, such caregivers become the reason a child is taught conditional love because of the lack of emotional understanding of the caregiver and the innate need to validate themselves externally by living through their children. They judge children for their grades and give them conditional love so they make all life decisions according to their choices and have no say over how they should live their lives in the first place.

The school, university, careers, and spouses of such adults are decided by their caregivers. If children choose to live on their own terms, they are always called difficult, selfish, insensitive, and inconsiderate. Such children are constantly shamed, bullied, gaslighted, emotionally manipulated, and screamed at as they act as a threat to their caregiver's societal hierarchy of validation for making different life choices that do not match the caregiver's vision.

Such caregivers never see the child as an individual entity but as an extension of themselves who will carry forward their moral values, beliefs, traditions, norms, surname, and societal baton to fit into the so-called man-made social construct. In families, the legacy of herd mentality and decisions based on groupthink are encouraged, accepted, and validated. A child will do anything to get that validation, so they sacrifice their own needs and feelings by abandoning their passion for living life on their own terms, giving up on themselves and handing over power over their major life decisions to their caregiver by letting them dictate their life choices.

Such adults are always emotionally dependent on their caregivers for external validation to feel good about themselves. They end up as emotional toddlers with unhealthy nervous regulation systems in adult bodies by becoming emotional slaves to their own caregivers. These adults who do this to themselves do not realize they have turned into exact mouthpieces and replicas of their caregivers as adults and have no individuality. They act, think, and believe the same things their caregivers do due to heavy conditioning of their belief system, have the same psychological triggers, and are no longer emotionally independent or evolving individually.

This is a family construct of all joint families; people resemble each other like robots with no individual identity or personality and are heavily emotionally dependent on each other for external validation. Such setups only promote toxic co-dependency, groupthink behaviour, self-sacrificing behaviour, self-neglect, self-abandonment, disrespect, and emotional dependency due to a false sense of the societal construct of a happy family.

The whole concept of family and community we build is based on external factors, not on human values of empathy, love, kindness, care, selflessness, emotional safety, loyalty, and belongingness. That is why we get along with only a few family members, relatives, siblings, and caregivers. Our emotional dependency is so intertwined as adults that people who are not healthy for our nervous system make us feel disrespected, emotionally unsafe, self-centred, and only have empathy towards their own emotional needs. We are forced to tolerate and deal with them regularly because of our distorted perception that family is everything.

When it comes to friendship, we are free to form friendships based on our human values, and with time, if we grow apart or our values are no longer aligned, we have that freedom to end it by putting our emotional needs and safety first. Such dogmatic structure of binding people together who are not emotionally healthy for each other is why many humans still suffer.

Due to our ingrained and societal belief system of bonding based on man-made relationships of relatives—based on surnames, shared tradition, culture, nation, caste, colour, and societal standing—we are conditioned to accept such people as our own due to our biological connection to them. However, no one teaches us to cut off such people who have left us emotionally traumatized and fearful and made us stop loving ourselves as children because they saw us as extensions of themselves and felt ashamed if we chose not to become their followers or worship them as caregivers by wanting to be our own person.

No one teaches us that if you feel emotionally unsafe in someone's company, that is your body's signal to protect yourself from them. Even if we are gaslighted as adults and believe they wanted the best for us, our bodies will remember the trauma, suffering, and harm they caused. We will abandon, disrespect, and hate ourselves internally if we ignore it. Such emotional gaslighting plays out in terms of love-hate relationships with such caregivers, siblings, spouses, partners, friendships, and relatives as we give in and accept our role in their lives by self-abandonment due to heavy conditioning of the mind.

We need to learn to honour ourselves by building a healthy relationship with our inner child and slowly learning to trust, respect, and value our existence as humans. We are not born to play the role of someone's son or daughter and carry forward their legacy of the man-made construct of a happy family by marrying and creating offspring. We are not born as individuals to be part of someone else's dream, family, business, or community by taking up their emotional responsibility. All adults are responsible for their own emotions and self first.

We always had and will always have a choice to establish boundaries with others to have a healthy relationship with ourselves. We always have free will to exercise and choose ourselves by overcoming the psychological barriers of the saviour complex within us to save others or wait to be saved by others. It is not our role or job to live for others but for ourselves, as our time is limited and precious.

Anyone who loves us unconditionally will never judge us for our choices and will always provide us with an emotionally safe space to live authentically on our own terms as children and adults. We need to let go of resentment, expectations, and emotional co-dependency from anyone who has not provided us the unconditional love we deserved as children. If it means detaching our emotions to become emotionally healthy and heal our wounds, learn to put yourself first by honouring your feelings and self-respect.

We always have a choice to build a family of emotionally healthy and safe people who always want the best for us and accept us for who we are without trying to change a single thing about us. Those people are your real family; just because someone gave birth to you does not mean they can love you unconditionally and always want the best for you. Due to their own generational trauma, they only wish to do what is acceptable in society for them because they are conditioned always to be emotionally dependent on others to feel good about themselves.

Such people will always try to control you and your choices to feel emotionally safe because of their own unhealed nervous system.

You are not here to follow in the footsteps of your caregiver, society, siblings, or relatives. Do not let others make your life decisions as adults by constantly gaslighting you emotionally with their so-called best intentions of turning you into an emotionally dependent robot that acts, thinks, and functions just like them to belong and be accepted. The norms, customs, and traditions they ask you to follow have always been man-made. They have nothing to do with the human value system but are solely based on man-made beliefs that make them feel united and emotionally safe and provide them with an external identity.

Your identity is of a human first, based on core human values; the rest are all belief systems that put us in boxes. The moment we accept and identify such belief systems as our own by making our surname, caste, family name, traditions, culture, norms, rules, and nation our core identity by attaching our emotions to it, we stop growing emotionally as adults by accepting the societal division of boxes, as we start to identify such man-made concepts as a false sense of emotional safety. It gets psychologically ingrained in our brains due to heavy conditioning as adults. Anything that harms it will always elicit fight-and-flight responses within us.

The dogmatic society thrives with such divisions by making humankind fight amongst each other in the name of nation, surname, religion, caste, culture, norms, and rules so that we never move beyond survival mode and enter our thriving era.

Public figures, brands, and celebrities keep taking advantage of our emotions by taking sides, creating wars, and showing how much they care about the divisions they made in the first place. Our psychological response has been their weapon to keep humankind divided so they can rule over us, cause damage to our mind and body, distract us with entertainment so we never emotionally heal as humans and become independent to see through all the lies, money constructs, and power plays they have made to keep us trapped as slaves in this modern world. We are so occupied with trivial matters through social media that we never focus on healing ourselves and becoming dependent on ourselves, to care for ourselves.

We must sit with ourselves and think first: are we ready for a relationship, and why are we seeking it? It is a setup for failure if the reason is based on age, religion, bank balance, designation, job security, purchasing power, properties, family name, caste, education, or co-dependency. Let me explain why: what do we do if we do not get along well with any friends and do not feel emotionally understood and safe as humans? With time, we end up cutting ties because, in their company, we felt emotionally drained, misunderstood, and disrespected. That is because we are in tune with how we feel emotionally around such people and have the freedom to put our emotional needs first when it comes to surrounding ourselves with people who make us feel safe as human beings.

We love having friends around who make us feel uplifted, wanted, understood, and needed by giving us a safe space to be ourselves in their company. We feel validated, understood, and accepted for who we are in their presence. Now, imagine emotional compatibility, safety, and security are not even parameters considered in this dogmatic society as significant factors in deciding if two humans are compatible. That is why we end up in toxic relationships where our childhood unhealed wounds flare up, and we accuse the other person of being emotionally unavailable to our needs.

The pain of unhealed trauma leads to such issues that no matter how much we try, our psychological wounds will keep showing up in our toxic behaviour until we learn how to take accountability and responsibility for creating a safe emotional space within us as adults by taking care of our own emotional needs first. Only then are we in a healthy emotional space to take responsibility for another human being in a partnership.

Chapter 13
Your Real Happily Ever After

We are taught that getting married means happily ever after. After the illusion wears off, it is another man-made societal goal designed not to allow you to think for yourself first. Marriage or partnership is not the goal of life, as reiterated by films, shows, society, caregivers, friends, or family. Our goal as humans has always been to discover ourselves first and focus on becoming the emotionally evolved version of ourselves internally by learning proper emotional regulation and healing from within.

We are supposed to clear and heal all the barriers within us that stop us from falling in love with our own company in solitude by living in a constant state of bliss, reinforcing positive perception of self and our environment, and achieving an emotionally healed nervous system that is no longer working in survival mode by producing cortisol caused by stress that our body accumulates because of our thinking patterns.

It also means living with a free mind that no longer needs any external distractions like phones, the internet, social media, celebrity watching, films, dating apps, surface-level connections, shows, going out, or travelling to escape and relax your unhealthy nervous system, developed due to heavy societal conditioning.

If we fall into the societal construct of marrying when we have not let go of our childhood emotional baggage, many issues of incompatibility or lack of emotional connection arise when surface-level attraction fades away. We still try to make marriage work by listening to everyone gaslighting us about how great the other person is. Despite the issues, we again try to make it work by having children and then start living for the children, just as our parents did. This, my friend, is what generational trauma is all about. We are always taught to seek love in others, and we tend to do that as adults by controlling others because we fear being alone and empty but are never taught to seek love from within.

No one tells us or teaches us how to love yourself unconditionally first so you can learn to pour into yourself before pouring into others. We eventually turn into the same controlling caregivers we feared and hated most because our emotional need to be safe was not honoured by ourselves as adults.

Marriage law in a dogmatic society revolves around money-related rights for property ownership, child custody, bank ownership, and surname transfer for some. It binds us so we feel a false sense of security. Then, if someone wants to get out of a relationship on paper, there is again a market setup that makes massive money from people discussing a private matter between two consenting individuals because they are no longer emotionally compatible or have not worked through their own emotional regulation issues, leading to an ending on bad terms. No one discusses the root cause of having such laws in place—that is, due to lack of emotional maturity and growth, the reason for marriage being a materialistic checklist of false sense of security and entitlement behaviour that comes from having an ego of ownership over a person.

No one tells you that most arranged marriages are giant traps because caregivers are trying to live through their child by blindly following the societal norm of finding a groom or bride for their child, as if they are shopping for a human being that fits the man-made false construct of religion, caste, bank balance, societal standing, surname, age, family background, height, and looks that will fit into their illusion of a perfect family, according to the societal hierarchy created by humankind.

These setups do not consider emotional compatibility or a healthy, regulated nervous system. Then, based on surface-level interactions, these adults fall in love by gaslighting themselves as they search for love, believing they found the right person, as the other person validated all the love chemicals of dopamine, serotonin, and oxytocin. Again, we depend on someone externally to feel complete and emotionally fulfilled without looking inward.

The same applies to many love marriages today where boundaries and emotional independence are not encouraged. Such relationships only promote co-dependency and a false sense of security because we have not regulated our emotions and dealt with ourselves enough to give that to ourselves internally. Two unhealed people coming together to setup a family just like their caregivers did, and they continue in this survival mode by brushing the emotional compatibility issues under the carpet because the honeymoon period of two people gaslighting each other by putting forward their best behaviour to impress each other comes off the table.

Their authentic selves emerge with time. Once they see each other for who they actually are, most of them no longer connect or like their spouses, and with time, respect goes out the window too. They fail to realize that they never approached each other as their authentic selves, as they had a goal in mind—marriage, as they were brainwashed into believing they had entered the right age to shop for the perfect groom or bride. This is also true for many relationships we see today. Resentment, disrespect, and lack of love have taken over in such setups.

The societal structure of groupthink forces people or at least gaslights people into believing that this is their life plan like everyone else's. No one is taught to learn emotional regulation, heal their emotional wounds, and love themselves unconditionally first because, in their eyes, the right age means they will be able to procreate and bear a child so the family's lineage can continue. Anyone who chooses themselves in such a society acts as a threat because if they do not procreate, their genetic line will end with that person. They cannot bear to live with that thought because they see their children as extensions of themselves and subconsciously feel entitled to own their life choices in the process.

If bank balance, looks, religion, culture, caste, family lineage, cars, degrees, having children, or social status are the parameters for happily ever after, why are we still having domestic violence, suicides, loneliness, emotional dependency, unhappy marriages, cheating, debauchery, marital rape, custody battles, and criminal court cases? We were told we would have a life partner, but most of us ended up being slaves for life to their issues that they refuse to heal or deal with.

Clearly, this model of marriages or relationships does not work when the love chemicals of oxytocin, endorphins, and serotonin wear off and slowly, with time, resentment emerges as the rose-coloured lens of seeing love through surface-level attraction and our belief system wears off. This is what conditional love looks like. We do this to ourselves because we are constantly taught to love conditionally in this society where our emotions are connected to external stimuli.

Let me just say that shopping for fancy brands, eating unhealthy foods, drinking, smoking, and indulging in surface-level connections for external validation are just forms of conditional love we provide ourselves because our dopamine receptors are hooked to those for survival. We have not been taught how to love ourselves unconditionally, and we are just going in circles, eventually questioning ourselves deep down: who am I? The relationship we seek, or are in, is a direct reflection of the love we have for ourselves.

Getting married and having children was never the goal of human beings as a species; our goal was always to fall in love unconditionally with ourselves first, by becoming emotionally healthy through our lessons in life—by reaching a balanced emotional state of being comfortable with the full spectrum of emotions from the inside. Marriage or relationships have always been a byproduct of falling in love with our self first and organically meeting someone on your life's journey. If one connects over a shared value system, with time they may enter an emotionally healthy partnership without any financial, emotional, or mental co-dependency.

True love is a union of two emotionally intelligent individuals with healthy, regulated nervous systems who share similar human values without co-dependency, and they see themselves and the world with the same perspective, making them emotionally, intellectually, and physically compatible. It has nothing to do with man-made constructs of belief systems based on nation, age, race, colour, creed, bank balance, surname, job titles, education, or purchasing power. If this were the case, then we would not have been so overpopulated as a planet that we are on the verge of exhausting our ecosystem, that supports life, by already making it unliveable.

Chapter 14
Knowledge of Brand Self

One must understand oneself as a brand in today's world if one is to understand oneself. You are not supposed to subscribe to or follow someone else's ideologies as a brand. Everyone tries to pitch themselves as superior and the best human beings to stand out, but we fail to realize that we must work alongside our values. All of us are mere mortals and equals in the eyes of the Creator. Once we understand this, we can easily understand that anyone trying to sell themselves as a product or brand is nothing but a narcissist attempting to sell themselves as a brand or shop to you to make you to become their follower.

This is a world of popularity where everyone is busy explaining why they are better human beings than other people to gain an upper hand of purchasing power over other human beings. Everyone is running a race to prove why they are better humans despite knowing very well that we all have the same values of kindness, love, empathy, selflessness, care, and so forth. All of us are blessed equally with these values, and we sell them to others to gain popularity, money, fame, and followers. Isn't it ironic? We need to do human things so we can do inhuman things like hoarding wealth despite seeing so many people suffer from lack of money to begin with.

Anyone trying to sell themselves as a brand by projecting their superiority complex instead of telling you that we are all equals with the same human values and deserve nothing but equal opportunities to shine and be the best version of ourselves is nothing but a fraudulent, selfish, and self-centred human being who only cares about themselves, their popularity, and their existence. All they are making us do is fight for their attention, when all we ever needed was our own attention to begin with.

Until we keep giving others—be it celebrities, idols, or any public figure—power over us by treating them as superior, idols, or god-like people, we will continue suffering due to our own perception of self and the world around us. We are the main character, brand, and person in our life's story. We need to keep it that way; we need to become obsessed with ourselves and continuously focus on evolving as humans based on our human values.

Remember this: how you perceive yourself is how you see the world because our world reflects how we see ourselves in our own eyes. The majority of the world will benefit from it if we do not know ourselves as adults, but the day we choose to work on and connect with our authentic selves, we have truly been born because—it is now that people cannot take us for a ride. We are no longer living in survival mode; we have entered thriving mode as we have accepted this vital information that we are the main character of our story and no one else can replace us and our existence.

We never attach a price to priceless things, be it our human values such as our ability to love, nurture, care, empathize, trust, experience freedom and joy, be grateful, kind, selfless, loyal, and compassionate towards ourselves, each other, animals, and our planet. Money was created to make trade easy, but now it is nefarious in creating a divide amongst humankind by creating a belief system to promote it through constant conditioning of the mind, body, and thoughts, creating massive barriers by turning our own minds against our values, by brainwashing us across centuries.

This promotes values based on fear, hatred, ego, apathy, rage, resentment, insecurity, unworthiness, self-loathing, revenge, worry, boredom, overthinking, anger, guilt, shame, envy, selfishness, greed, power, jealousy, self-doubt, and lack of confidence that keeps us inhuman and does not allow us to embrace our natural values as humans to embrace ourselves by practising humanity. The economic, national, political, religious, and racial divide has been formulated for success in ruling over humankind across centuries, to turn them into slaves so that such elites can keep ruling over humankind, animals, and our planet for their own selfish motives.

Exerting control through our purchasing power by owning expensive brands, homes, cars, land, and animals, creating a family, maintaining relationships, climbing up the money-based societal hierarchy, and flaunting things do not make us successful—but freeing our minds from such beliefs does! It removes us from being slaves to our conditioning and allows us to discover our true, authentic selves.

Chapter 15
Back to Being Human

The day we stop caring about other people's opinions, belief systems, and conditioning about how one should live their lives and care about others as humans is when we start moving towards unity. We have lived through thousands of years based on division—how about changing the narrative and focusing on connecting with others on a human level, no matter what their religion, country, social status, bank balance, colour, face, or body looks like?

The only thing in danger today is our humanity, as it is being exploited by greedy, selfish, manipulative, egoistic, power-hungry, and vain people who are fascist and always looking for opportunities to divide and rule through ideologies, by conditioning us across centuries through our belief systems. The moment we become fearless by escaping self-limiting beliefs about our capabilities, their walls and world created to serve selfish interests with no empathy towards humankind, nature, or animals will crumble like a house of cards!

Let's value trees, plants, animals, humans, water, ecology, and our planet. Be creative and learn the skills you always wanted to learn, but were constrained from pursuing them, as a slave in a cubicle, due to the conditioning that money is everything. We as humans are everything we need; we can love, create, empathize, care, and have minds that help us flourish and create the reality we want when we do things from our heart with love. This connection keeps our humanity alive as we can love and embrace each other, and the only thing that stops us is the barrier created by a society run by man-made money.

Do not let others' beliefs and societal constructs force you to change or adopt theirs. We, as humankind, are not here to merely exist and follow rules that no longer make sense to us just because someone said so. We are here to carve our identity based on who we truly are from the inside; to not believe in things that bind us but to believe in things that free our minds; to question anything and everything that no longer makes sense despite billions still following it like a herd; we are here to shape the shift of humankind, as individuals with our emotional connection to ourself and others.

A human being who knows who they are and is aware of their infinite potential. Let's go back to our ancient roots of what it was just to be human first and focus on evolving our minds to make this place better for everyone, be it humans, animals, or Earth itself. Let's focus on changing core beliefs by shedding them and accepting ourselves based on our values of kindness, empathy, love, care, and solitude, that always brought us peace.

Let's let go of the world of chaos where everyone is driven by ego, fear, greed, power, idol worship, money, hatred, jealousy, vanity, envy, and selfishness with zero consideration towards others. This stops us from embracing our humanity and connecting with our real, authentic selves due to heavy societal conditioning. Let's make a conscious decision to nurture and heal our thoughts and minds first by listening to our hearts, which binds all of us to being human first!

The world today is about achieving a successful life. It's about ticking off all the boxes of the same life checklist followed by everyone worldwide as a definition of a successful or well-lived life. Be it getting good grades, studying at the best university, having a well-paid career or business, marrying for looks first along with qualifications that fit human shopping, as one turns a certain age, having children, or retiring. Everyone is following the same template and running the race to tick everything off this list, as they are supposed to; anyone who does not follow the script or goes astray is bullied, criticized, or looked down upon in society and, in some cases, shunned for existing.

So how do you leave this never-ending race for life's checklist and focus on finding your purpose, you may ask? By discovering who you are. We all have a life's calling and a purpose that brings us contentment. But to speak the language of gratitude and love from the heart space, one needs to first feel emotionally safe and secure in their own company, when in solitude.

The moment the silence surrounding you feels like solitude and does not make you feel lonely, you are operating from your heart space by accepting yourself for who you are—the good, the bad, and the ugly. But to achieve this feat, you must let go of everything that stops you from being authentic. You must be comfortable with the uncomfortable, even if it means cutting people off for your self-respect.

The more you are aligned with human values, where you respect, love, honour, and trust yourself by always putting your emotional needs first, the more slowly you will become the best version of your authentic, real self. You become your best friend by shunning everything that no longer serves you, especially those living in survival mode, living off ego by maintaining the image of how they are perceived by others instead of being real in this dogmatic societal structure.

Such people will always have selective empathy; they will love, help, give trust, or be there for you only for their convenience or until they find it justified according to their logic. We cannot measure love; if someone does it and acts accordingly, let them go. Such people are always there for a good time and will be the first ones to bolt when you need them most because they are emotionally unavailable to themselves. They cannot give you what they do not have and have not learnt to give themselves.

End such chapters before your life becomes a sad story because of them. They are the roadblocks to your purpose; life is meant to be lived freely and on your own terms based on contentment. Never give anyone else power over you to make you feel bad about your own existence. We are here to experience all emotions and to own them. If someone cannot be there for you during bad times, they do not deserve to be with you during your best.

So how does one identify those living in survival mode so they can enter thriving mode? The first step would be to detach from anyone who is driven by ego, lives for their image, and constantly seeks to control others' perceptions. Such people do not know themselves and constantly seek validation, money, power, and authority. They are obsessed with ownership of materialistic things and being popular in their community or circle. They will be obsessed with all man-made things—festivals, religion, politics, or entertainment.

They would love to always talk about others and how great they are, all the time, to maintain their perception and image in the minds of others. Their identities are solely based on how others perceive them because they have fragile egos. They will always play the victim card and seek empathy from others by claiming that the world has always wronged them, whilst hiding their part or role in their stories. They want sympathy because they are emotionally dependent on others to seek validation about how nice they are.

They would be beyond selfish, never making their own children emotionally independent by never teaching them even survival skills, so that their children would not stop needing them in life. Anyone who is authentic will not have an image to maintain; such people will always be honest with you, and you will always be loved for who you are. Those are your real people and the ones you should seek in life as your confidants. They are the ones who will always stand by you during your trying times and will love you for who you are, be it good, bad, or ugly.

They have learnt in life to accept themselves wholly, unapologetically, and truthfully. They stand tall based on their values of kindness, empathy, selflessness, compassion, love, and all the good qualities that make us human.

The moment you start to take accountability and responsibility for your life instead of questioning "Why me?", see how your life slowly begins to change. How we think, feel, and view ourselves and the world is directly proportional to our emotional growth and intelligence. Our perception plays a key role in how we see ourselves and everyone else. Society will always try to distort it as it fears the unknown and is constantly brainwashed to play it safe and stick to the tried and tested model of slavery.

We, as humans, are here to lead ourselves towards the life we want based on inner contentment. We were never followers as a species. All of us are unique and one of a kind, and no one on this planet can ever replace us! Anyone who tells you that you are ordinary is delusional. We were born extraordinary and can achieve and be anything we ever wanted as humans. Never strive to be someone else; always focus on being the best version of yourself—someone who is emotionally evolved, authentic, and real, grounded in human values and self-learned beliefs that are not swayed by others.

Chapter 16
Affirmations

Here's a list of affirmations that is going to help in the process of regulating both negative and positive emotions based on our life experiences.

No Longer Hate Self

I no longer hate myself because:

1. I realize my caregiver projected their hatred, blame, and shame onto me.
2. I now realize they transferred their feelings onto me to fit societal standards for validation, which had nothing to do with my true self.
3. I am not an extension of my caregiver; I am my own person with the freedom to choose my life.
4. I've realized that everyone is unique and that worth isn't tied to appearance. Society's flawed beauty standards made me feel inferior

from a young age, teaching me to compare myself to unrealistic ideals. Perfection is an illusion; our humanity lies in our imperfections. We should prioritize what feels right instead of aimlessly chasing societal expectations.

5. I am not my marks, school, university, career, salary, car, waist size, or bank balance. I am a human with different emotions, and I am allowed to feel them.
6. My self-judgement and hatred from childhood hindered my growth. As an adult, I take full responsibility for my life and recognize that these deep-rooted beliefs are not mine. I know I am stronger than that.
7. I let go and forgive those who brought me darkness, which has helped me find my light. I'm grateful for the lessons that encourage self-discovery. I realize that holding onto resentment gives others power over my thoughts and contributes to my suffering. The right choice is to be a better person and move on.
8. I choose peace over self-harming thoughts. I recognized that without taking ownership of my life, I risked becoming like my abuser or a narcissist trapped in self-hatred. While I wasn't taught self-love, I am now committed to supporting myself and addressing the damage caused by others. This journey is for my happiness and healing.
9. I realize that my attraction to emotionally unavailable partners stems from my childhood experiences with conditional love and projection of hatred. It's not anyone else's responsibility to love me if I don't love myself.
10. I refuse to remain a child in an adult's body and am learning to grow in an environment that allows me to thrive. Though I sometimes fall

back into toxic patterns, I understand that progress takes time. I'm committed to investing in myself daily and believe in my ability to create the emotional support I've always sought.

11. I'm working on owning my voice by accepting all parts of myself, especially those I once hated, and treating them compassionately. I recognize the need to take responsibility for my thoughts and beliefs, which often do not reflect my true self. While disagreement may evoke memories of feeling misunderstood, I've outgrown those dynamics. I'm willing to let go of anyone who doesn't respect me, as self-respect is my top priority.
12. I don't blame anyone for not choosing me as a friend in school, university, or at work. I realized that I first needed to be my own friend. I can't achieve that while hating myself or seeking validation from others to feel good.
13. I recognize that years of conditioning have turned me into my own worst enemy. As an adult, I'm committed to eliminating the negative thoughts that prevent me from genuinely discovering and loving myself.
14. I realize that the critical voice within me stems from a caregiver who loved me conditionally. Everyone interprets love differently; some are willing to learn, while others aren't. Accepting this has changed me for the better. I no longer get upset when I feel unheard or emotionally unsafe. I understand that people perceive things from their limited perspectives, and not everyone is open to learning, growing, or reflecting on their role in their own or others' suffering.
15. I unnecessarily tortured myself, depriving myself of my own affections and then emotionally eating or purging to make myself

feel good. It led to a constant loop of unhealthy choices as an adult, such as substance addiction, while trying to cope emotionally.

16. I've always judged myself by confining myself to a limiting box created by my own self-limiting beliefs. This box has nothing to do with my true capabilities. Instead of opening the box and exploring within myself, I allowed others to define who I should be.
17. I realize that my self-critical voice caused me to give away my power to others, allowing them to mistreat me in friendships, relationships, and family dynamics. My desire to be liked and please others overshadowed my self-love, respect, and worth. This need for validation led me to abandon my authentic self as I sought external approval to feel good inside. Consequently, I placed others above myself, relying on them for my emotional needs.
18. I no longer judge myself. I recognize that I was shaped by a society focused on external validation, where people seek approval from one another instead of learning to validate themselves. We often base our worth on external factors like careers, degrees, relationships, looks, and money rather than internal qualities such as kindness, love, compassion, sincerity, loyalty, and helpfulness.
19. I am committed to healing my inner child, who learned to place worth in the wrong areas. While I recognize that we need money to function in this world, I understand that external factors do not define who we are inside. Our thoughts shape our reality, so I'm dedicated to showing compassion and speaking to myself with love.
20. I no longer feel the need to escape my self-made prison of negative thoughts by going on holiday. I recognize that humans are here to learn and make mistakes. I no longer judge myself or others, understanding that we all do our best to survive.

21. My goal is no longer just survival in this man-made society. I see myself as the protagonist of my life, with no one else holding power over me. I am the captain of my ship, and I will navigate unknown territories with self-love, compassion, and trust, moving forward with positivity.
22. Though the fear of not being good enough may still haunt me occasionally, I know that with resilience and by refusing to let those voices hold power over me, I will ultimately become my authentic self—the person I was always meant to be.

No Longer Blame Myself

I no longer blame myself because:

1. Throughout childhood, I did my best to survive and make the most of life. It took time to realize that the mistreatment and insults I experienced stayed with me because my body carried that trauma. I felt disrespected and hurt when I was ridiculed and bullied by my caregiver for not being like them.
2. I now understand that blaming myself for my capabilities in a man-made world designed to keep me constrained is not my fault. I fell into the same trap as others, where learning new skills to nurture my creativity felt like an alien concept. I was trained to be a slave to this system, judging myself for getting caught in a model that equates more money with safety, control, individuality, and power.
3. I no longer feel pressured to please others and am comfortable with people not liking me for who I am. I recognize that not everyone has my best interests at heart, and I'm comfortable cutting off relationships—whether friendships or family—if they

don't support my self-growth. This process often involves crying and feeling misunderstood, especially by those from whom I seek emotional support. Accepting people for who they are helps break the cycle of toxicity. Grieving that loss is essential, but those wounds can be filled with hope and optimism over time.

4. We always have the strength to distance ourselves from toxic people, but it's harder when they are loved ones. As adults, we must evaluate who makes us feel safe and recognize that some may be beyond saving. Ultimately, we deserve the love and acceptance we never received.
5. I realize it was not my fault that my caregiver preferred to blame others and chose me because I was the most expressive and empathetic child. My independence and refusal to follow their outdated rules and beliefs threatened them, as they wanted to break me in the same way they had been treated. I became a challenge to them because I wouldn't conform to the identity they held so tightly.
6. I now have compassion for my caregivers, understanding that they were never taught to love themselves. Unhealed people often hurt others, and I chose not to follow in their footsteps; instead, I sought peace. I focused on my healing and reclaimed my power, revealing my caregiver's struggles with external validation and their desire to be liked by others. It's not entirely their fault; many are caught up in pursuing popularity and fame, seeking validation to feel good, as they dislike their own company. Instead of engaging with their thoughts in solitude, they seek distractions to avoid facing themselves.
7. I no longer engage in behaviours that harm me. I take accountability for my actions and set firm boundaries with those who make my

inner child feel unsafe. I recognize that I am responsible for myself and no longer blame others for the harm they caused. My past experiences as a young adult stemmed from my lack of self-respect.

8. I no longer blame myself for failed surface-level relationships or friendships. I understand that people, including myself, can only love based on their capacity to love themselves. I recognize that one must be emotionally stable to seek emotionally stable relationships. We truly reap what we sow.
9. I realize it's not my job to base my life on my caregivers' choices. They made those choices to seek happiness and societal validation or to relive dreams their parents stifled. Their lives revolved around the belief that money is everything. True fulfilment comes from developing skills, following passions, and becoming emotionally intelligent. Money is just a byproduct, not something to live for.
10. I no longer base my worth on material success. While these are part of life, they don't define me. I have the freedom to live authentically. Being true to myself and passionately pursuing my interests allows me to live the life I want and do what I love most.
11. I now understand that anything that happens to me only occurs when I allow it. I no longer permit others to mistreat me, nor do I remain in emotionally or physically abusive relationships. I have learned to recognize my values and have made peace with my past actions, viewing them as lessons for my growth as a human being.
12. I'm comfortable having difficult conversations with those who disrespect me, knowing that not everyone understands the importance of boundaries. I do this because I'm accountable for keeping my inner child safe, and that responsibility rests with me alone.

13. I am responsible for reassuring myself when I make mistakes and treating myself with love and compassion. Mistakes are part of the learning process, and we should focus on growth rather than obsessing over results, grades, or errors. No one is born an expert in their passions; we're all here to seek knowledge and experience. Enjoying the journey and not becoming attached to the outcome is essential.
14. I trust my inner instinct to guide me in making the right decisions, and I no longer blame myself. Over time, I've become my best friend and cheerleader. The conscious mind often acts like an overactive brain, clinging to control and repeating childhood narratives programmed to seek danger. Our minds can only perceive what our thoughts dictate: if negative, we find countless reasons to be fearful; if positive, we uncover many reasons to be grateful. As adults, it's our responsibility to shift our perception of ourselves, as the world around us reflects how we see ourselves within.
15. I live on a planet of free will, where it's the basic need of any human to live the life they want to the fullest.
16. I no longer feel ashamed of my identity or the choices that brought me here. I recognize that society often measures worth based on material success, which leads to unnecessary pressure and comparison among individuals.
17. I've realized that boundaries are subjective, shaped by the family dynamics we grow up in rather than being taught explicitly. As an adult, it's my responsibility to communicate what I am comfortable with. I should never feel guilty or ashamed for expressing my basic need to feel safe in my environment.

18. It's acceptable to make mistakes; we're here to witness and experience life. We're all learning and trying things for the first time. Instead of feeling ashamed about what I don't know, I feel comfortable asking questions to educate myself better.
19. I recognize that feelings of guilt and shame were instilled in me by my caregiver's disapproval of my marks, clothes, friendships, hobbies, and lifestyle choices. These messages led me to believe I was at fault for their shame, causing me to develop a habit of seeking approval and validation, often at the expense of my interests and well-being.
20. I chose to break this pattern that influenced my choice of partners. I now realize that by dating emotionally unavailable people, I was attempting to fix them and seek their approval rather than focusing on healing my inner child myself.
21. I made those choices because I was hurt and sought validation for my feelings. Now I understand that I am responsible for validating myself as an adult, and it's no one else's job.
22. By emotionally regulating and acknowledging the hurt I caused, I am taking steps towards feeling comfortable in my own skin and enjoying my own company.
23. The body shaming I experienced in childhood reflected others' insecurities and had nothing to do with my true self.
24. I release the past hurt and recognize that boundaries are essential for my safety. It's crucial to acknowledge that caregivers can only love from their perspective. Until I accept this, I can't move beyond seeking their validation. As an adult, I realize that their view of the world is distorted, and I can no longer afford to adopt that mindset.
25. I feel safe in my body and surroundings because I trust myself to care of myself. Vulnerability is my strength and superpower. While

moving mountains may take a village, I know my willpower is stronger than my fears. With time and practice, I can reprogram my thoughts and reparent myself. My nervous system will learn that it no longer needs to stay in fight-or-flight mode. I can ease psychological distress by letting go of beliefs that blind me and hinder my emotional growth. I recognize that these narratives stem from my conditioning and societal pressures rather than celebrating our unique quirks and humanity.

26. I'm now comfortable with all my emotions, feeling free to be myself and connect with others as humans first.
27. Why not laugh when we stumble instead of feeling embarrassed about what others think? If pandas worried about what other pandas thought, imagine the chaos! They don't care what other pandas think; they just embrace who they are.

No Longer Abandon Myself

I no longer abandon myself because:

1. Earlier, I put others before myself because I needed to help people for external validation to feel good about myself.
2. I was uncomfortable with conflict because I had subconsciously learnt that prioritizing my needs was selfish, while putting others first was selfless.
3. I recognize that self-sacrificing behaviour is often celebrated in society, particularly for women, who are expected to manage household duties like cooking and cleaning while also maintaining careers.
4. I empathize with women trapped in a patriarchal society, where they often lack a voice in crucial decisions like marriage, household

responsibilities, or career paths. This lack of free will can lead to profound self-abandonment, as they seek validation by conforming to others' expectations instead of honouring their own desires and choices.

5. The lack of control in one's life can lead to deep depression, often causing women to seek fulfilment through their children, repeating patterns established by previous generations. I'm grateful to be a cycle breaker, prioritizing my well-being, security and living authentically rather than perpetuating these harmful dynamics.
6. I recognize that I always have the choice to leave unhealthy relationships, whether they're with friends, partners, or family. By prioritizing myself and my boundaries, I embrace my role as the creator and writer of my life and destiny.
7. I realize that attachments can be harmful. It's important to love myself and those around me freely, without tolerating abuse or disrespect simply out of attachment. True love includes respect and healthy boundaries.
8. I release anyone who no longer serves me or has negative intentions. My priority is feeling secure and safe. I take full accountability for my life; while others can advise, I am in control.
9. I listen to advice but trust my instincts to make decisions. I no longer let others dictate my choices, big or small.
10. I can only form healthy relationships when I love myself unconditionally and enjoy my own company. If I rely on external factors—like money, looks, or status—for validation, I'll continue to abandon my needs and blame others for mistreatment. My struggle to be alone has led to unhealthy choices that compromise

my mental peace and self-respect. I commit to working on myself, knowing that a strong relationship with myself will positively impact my relationships with others.

11. You attract what you embody. How I see myself is mirrored in my relationships, whether with family or friends. My goal now is to cultivate love within—being kind, caring, and compassionate towards myself. When I feel whole, I can share that love freely with others.
12. I've stopped connecting with rags-to-riches stories that promote unrealistic optimism. While inspiring, these narratives often lead us to chase external validation instead of pursuing our true passions. They can make us abandon our authentic dreams for a superficial ideal of success.

No Self-Destructive Behaviour

I no longer indulge in self-destructive behaviour because:

1. I respect myself and my body, and anyone who values me only for my looks doesn't deserve a place in my life. Society often prioritizes vanity over genuine connection, leading to harmful behaviours like extreme dieting and cosmetic surgery. We tend to objectify ourselves in the quest for validation, overlooking the importance of emotional well-being. True healing comes from within, and we should focus on nurturing our true selves and fostering meaningful relationships that uplift us.
2. I've recognize the unhealthy behaviours and patterns I developed as survival skills to cope in a chaotic environment that left my inner child feeling unsafe.

3. I now recognize that my worth comes from within, defined by my kindness, love, empathy, and generosity—not by brands, cars, bank balances, or the achievements of those around me. Each person's uniqueness is what truly makes them valuable.
4. I respect my body and myself as a person. I no longer turn to unhealthy food for comfort, recognizing it was a way to cope with unregulated feelings. I now understand what harms and nourishes me, and I appreciate my internal beauty, which shines through externally.
5. I no longer engage with content that harms my mental state; I focus on positive news that fosters genuine human connections. I celebrate others for their kindness, loyalty, love, and care.
6. I seek out people who inspire me to be a better human, rejecting the illusion of comparison. I recognize that I am the main character in my life, and my goal is to become the best version of myself in my own eyes.
7. I choose clothes that boost my confidence, prioritizing comfort and sustainability over labels. I prefer garments that are eco-friendly and fully recyclable.
8. I no longer crave processed foods; I choose fresh fruits and vegetables that nourish my body. I listen to what my body needs, breaking free from relying on processed, chemically infused foods.
9. I am mindful of my actions and their impact on those around me. I avoid plastics and any products that are harmful to myself or the environment, opting for natural alternatives whenever possible.
10. I realize that the chaos I lived in was largely a creation of my mind. It stemmed from my unwillingness to let go of the past and my constant focus on the future, which fuelled my obsessive thinking.

11. I understand that I can only control my thoughts and actions; how others behave is a reflection of them, not of me.
12. How I view life is entirely up to me. If I focus on the negative, I will be the source of my own suffering.
13. I recognize that past experiences often lead to self-doubt and affect my confidence. Some days, my mind resists my heart's reassurance that everything will be fine. It clings to past patterns, predicting failure and warning me of danger, much like in our primitive era. This mindset is self-destructive, rooted in societal teachings that undermine my abilities. I am dedicated to unlearning this pattern, no matter how long it takes.
14. Some days, I may struggle to stick to my plans or believe in myself, and that's acceptable. For so long, caregivers, teachers, and others told me I wasn't good enough. I've realized that their judgements were often based on comparisons rather than recognizing my unique capabilities. This mindset reflects a herd mentality I'm working to break free from.
15. From my experiences, I've realized that fear is the main thing holding me back. While my mind tries to protect me from harm, it often defaults to the belief that things will go wrong. This conditioning has made me hesitant to embrace the unknown, clinging to familiar patterns. I understand I must challenge this mindset and start looking forward to new possibilities rather than relying solely on what feels safe and familiar.
16. My childhood hypervigilance, developed to navigate an unsafe environment, has turned me into an adult who overthinks every situation. I often fixate on worst-case outcomes, believing they're

inevitable because that's how things have always been for me. This thinking pattern keeps me trapped in fear, and I recognize that I need to break free from it to embrace new possibilities.

17. My brain often convinces me to hold back, suggesting that good things never happen to me. I create a false persona to protect myself, presenting an image of how I want others to see me. My mind tells me it's safer not to be my true self, even though this leads to loneliness. Acknowledging these patterns is the first step towards change.
18. I'm beginning to accept that I can be my own worst enemy if I don't check myself in time. Getting caught in negative thought patterns that fuel my overthinking is easy. As an adult, it's my responsibility to identify and challenge the beliefs I adopted in childhood that don't reflect my true self.
19. As a child, I learnt to hide whenever I was disappointed. It felt soothing and safe, like a bunker during a war. But as I grew older, I realized I was still following that pattern, avoiding the world instead of exploring it. I kept fighting for survival despite changing circumstances and was no longer helpless. It's time to step out of that bunker and embrace new experiences.
20. We often think of society's markers—careers, homes, money, cars—as the ultimate goals, but they're merely byproducts of a more profound journey. We're here to discover ourselves and our unique light. Each of us is special, and instead of aspiring to be like celebrities or leaders, we should strive to be the best version of ourselves. No one is a god; when we elevate others to that status, we give them power over us. We mustn't identify with labels that diminish our humanity. True worth lies in our capacity for empathy, love, kindness, and care. That's the essence of who we are.

21. Doubting ourselves and fixating on outcomes are forms of self-sabotage, often rooted in fear of the unknown. Our minds prioritize safety, a lesson ingrained in us from childhood through choices about schools, careers, and more. Those who dare to pursue different paths are often shunned or labelled unrealistic. This societal pressure can be a nightmare for dreamers striving to be authentic. Focusing on potential adverse outcomes creates barriers that keep me from pursuing my true desires. My fight-or-flight response, designed to protect me, often leads to assumptions of danger that hold me back from what I want.
22. I've become aware of these patterns and recognize that I engage in them to create a sense of safety. I'm learning not to self-loathe anymore; I embrace my journey and acknowledge my worth. Each step I take towards understanding myself brings me closer to genuine self-acceptance and growth.
23. It is acceptable to make mistakes. We are not perfect and were never supposed to be perfect. Imperfection is the trait that makes us human, as we are here to learn and grow.
24. The idea of perfection is an illusion rooted in childhood wounds that pressure us to conform and adopt socially acceptable personas. We're taught to be polite, please others, and prioritize their needs, leading us to suppress our true selves. Deviating from this mould often labels us as "difficult," trapping us in a cycle where we never fully explore who we are. Breaking free from these constraints and embracing our authentic selves is essential.
25. Being bullied in childhood for things beyond your control was profoundly unfair. It's empowering to recognize that your healing

is your responsibility as an adult. By letting go of resentment and forgiving those who may not have known better, you're prioritizing your mental well-being. Holding onto that pain only hinders your emotional growth. Ultimately, putting yourself first is an act of self-love and a crucial step towards moving forward. Your peace matters more than the hurtful actions of others.

26. Chasing perfection truly is like pursuing a mirage. The endless cycle of striving for an ideal body, accumulating wealth, or achieving status only leads to emptiness. Living in survival mode creates a relentless race—school, work, marriage, retirement—without ever genuinely enjoying life. Celebrating superficial milestones and showcasing curated happiness on social media isn't genuine living. True joy doesn't come from external validation or material success; it arises from within. The quest for perfection often blinds us to our own worth. Instead of measuring our value against societal standards, we should focus on what brings us authentic joy and fulfilment.
27. It's heartbreaking to think about how bullying can shape our inner dialogue. The harsh judgements we face as children can become the narratives we repeat to ourselves as adults. It's crucial to recognize that these negative voices aren't our true selves but reflections of others' cruelty. We can change this inner narrative by practising self-compassion and kindness. Instead of internalizing the hurt, we can nurture our curiosity and love for ourselves, just as we did when we were young. By being mindful of how we speak to ourselves, we can reclaim our worth and cultivate a more positive self-image.
28. It's so common to focus on perceived flaws when we look in the mirror, often driven by societal standards and the influence of

celebrity culture. These negative thoughts can overshadow the unique beauty we all possess. Instead of letting those critical voices take control, we can embrace every part of ourselves, including what we've been taught to dislike. It's about practising self-love and compassion, recognizing that our worth isn't defined by appearance or societal expectations. By rejecting those harmful narratives and appreciating our bodies as they are, we can reclaim our power and find confidence in our authenticity.

29. I know the need to get external validation from owning brands and following celebrity culture for my aspiration to be wealthy has been the reason for my limited self-perception. All the self-loathing stemmed from the fact that I couldn't afford the luxury of owning brands and homes in prominent locations. I was focusing my life decisions on a false sense of security.
30. We are set up for failure if we do not have a purpose and consistently follow a plan to make money. The things we didn't even identify with as children are everything we want as adults. If this is not conditioning, what is?
31. Self-loathing stems from feelings of inadequacy, but we can all learn, grow, and feel—qualities that transcend education, grades, careers, or wealth. Society's hierarchy creates inequality, but our true emotional intelligence lies in our ability to feel and think as humans. Clinging to a self-image based on external factors leads to a distorted reality, disconnecting us from our authentic selves.
32. Nature did not create money; it provided free resources like food, water, and air to foster community. Despite our intelligence, we've often used it to oppress the vulnerable, creating a false sense of

entitlement and slavery. Our identities and values are shaped by divisions based on borders, religion, and wealth. We own nothing; societal structures promote ownership as security but perpetuate inequality and fear, preventing us from realizing our true potential. Identity cards and government laws enforce conformity, limiting our freedom to explore who we are.

No Longer Self-Doubt

I no longer doubt myself because:

1. I now understand that when I doubt my abilities to handle life's events, I give my power to others. Recognizing this helps me reclaim my strength and confidence.
2. I can always welcome good advice, but I should stick to what I want.
3. Life is a journey of trial and error, where the focus should be on learning, not judgement. From childhood, we've been conditioned to judge ourselves based on marks, looks, and societal expectations rather than embracing our unique experiences.
4. Unlearning deep-seated conditioning can be challenging, but it's essential for my mental health. I trust my abilities to navigate challenges, even when solutions aren't immediately apparent. Each step forward is a testament to my growth.
5. I trust myself to set boundaries so that my kindness and selflessness are not taken for granted. I'm here to honour my humanity, not to cater to selfish or toxic people. I recognize that I cannot change others; I prioritize healing myself first. Only then can I truly support and uplift others.
6. I surround myself with people who offer love and kindness, giving me the space to grow and be myself without judgement. I deserve

to treat myself with that same compassion. Instead of relying solely on others for confidence, I can learn from them how to cultivate it within myself by taking accountability for my own life's journey.

7. A biased society harms everyone by pitting genders against each other, often leading to a constant struggle for dominance. I refuse to let these roles dictate who I am. Ultimately, we are all human, and the principles of kindness and respect apply to everyone, regardless of gender. It's societal beliefs and constructs that create biases, often trapping us in unhealthy situations out of fear of judgement. I realize that others are not accountable for my life—I must take responsibility for my choices. If I need support to break free from these man-made constraints, I am committed to seeking it. My well-being comes first; I trust everything else will align in time.
8. Staying in an unhappy marriage "for the children" doesn't serve anyone. Children need to see healthy, happy parents, not just the presence of both. I can create a life that reflects my values by prioritizing my well-being and setting healthy boundaries. When I show my children that choosing happiness and seeking fulfilment is acceptable, I empower them to do the same. We all can develop our skills and recognize our self-worth, which allows us to navigate life's challenges confidently. Choosing to move forward rather than remaining stuck in a situation teaches resilience and the importance of making choices that honour our true selves.
9. I must cultivate unconditional self-love before seeking partners, friendships, or relationships. The people I attract will mirror the love and acceptance I give myself. To experience healthy love from others, I need to embark on a journey of self-discovery and self-acceptance. As I learn to love myself fully, my self-doubts will

gradually fade, bringing me closer to my authentic self. This inner work is essential for building meaningful connections with others.

10. I no longer doubt my ability to love, heal, and accept myself. I recognize my worth and am excited to discover my authentic self. Anything that hinders this journey must go. My commitment to myself is my most important commitment in life.
11. My journey may be challenging and unexpected, but I know it's mine to navigate.

No Longer Self-Centred and Gaslighting Myself

I no longer am self-centred and gaslighting myself because:

1. I recognize that self-centredness has become a coping mechanism in our society. I see how I, too, have sometimes grown desensitized to the suffering around me—wars, poverty, cruelty—caring mostly for those I personally know. In doing so, I've distanced myself from a deeper sense of empathy and from the emotional connection that binds us as human beings.
2. I realize that fear often silences me when I should speak up. I've been conditioned to see suffering through fragmented lenses—race, class, geography—and these divisions have shaped how I relate to the world. I now understand that this conditioning began in my early years, when my value was tied to achievements, beliefs, and conformity. Today, I notice how that same search for worth continues through followers, wealth, and appearances. I recognize the emptiness that lies beneath these external measures.
3. I see how I've sometimes sought validation by being close to the powerful or well-known. I believed that proximity to fame made

me special. But I realize now this desire came from a place of inner lack. I forgot that celebrities are human too, and that placing them on pedestals only reinforces a system where inequality grows. I recognize that money, though created by humans, now controls us, distracting us from simpler, more equitable ways of living and connecting.

4. I acknowledge that I've often prioritized my own emotional pain, seeking reassurance rather than understanding. I see how fear has shaped my boundaries and kept me from deeper emotional intimacy. I realize that avoiding vulnerability has limited my ability to regulate emotions and fully feel them. I am learning that facing my feelings is not weakness—but freedom.
5. I realize I never built trust with myself, always making decisions based on my caregivers' opinions rather than my feelings. This created a disconnect between my mind, body, and emotions, leading to trauma and difficulties in emotional regulation. I learnt to bottle up my feelings, prioritizing others over myself, which resulted in an unhealthy relationship with myself.
6. The need to escape myself has been a recurring theme in my life, reinforced by societal structures that limit our ability to think for ourselves. Everything feels preplanned, with constant subtle advice and gestures guiding our decisions, leaving little room for personal reflection.
7. I now realize that my lack of confidence in my judgement has driven me to seek external validation. Fears of unfavourable outcomes led me to stick to familiar, societally approved paths, with many examples to follow. This fear of the unknown has prevented me from embracing what truly brings me contentment and peace.

8. I commit to being myself, even if it means losing important people in my life—they may come around with time and healthy boundaries.
9. I must prioritize my feelings over others' opinions when making decisions. It's acceptable to disagree and have uncomfortable conversations. I'm learning to do this instead of avoiding conflict and neglecting myself. I must respect myself first and stop betraying my feelings to please others.

No Longer Self-Judgemental

I am no longer self-judgemental because:

1. I understand that I am the main character of my storyline, and no one can take my place, whether I like it or not. I might as well take ownership of my existence.
2. My world revolves around me because I am the one who lives in my head 24/7 with my thoughts. My job is to make it the most loving, acceptable, and safe place for myself.
3. The need to be liked should not override my self-respect in any situation or with anyone because I need to look myself in the eyes and feel proud for existing. It is my sole job to ensure that I am proud of myself.
4. That inner critical voice in my head is something borrowed from my critical parent, who suffered from the conditioning of perfection and always saw the glass as half empty because their parent didn't appreciate them.
5. I am choosing to break the generational trauma by working on my self-perception because I understand that how I view myself is what the world will reflect back to me.

6. I am learning to prioritize my emotional needs instead of continuously putting others before myself. This shift is vital for fostering self-respect and personal well-being.
7. It's crucial to unlearn the unhealthy patterns that cause us to prioritize others' feelings over our own, particularly in environments dominated by narcissistic dynamics where one person's needs overshadow the collective.
8. I recognize that emotional growth is a continuous journey, not restricted by age. Understanding ourselves and honouring our feelings is a lifelong process that can occur at any stage of life.
9. Ultimately, my responsibility is not to ensure others feel emotionally safe at the expense of my well-being. Instead, I must create an environment where I feel secure and validated in every situation.

Self-Awareness

I am self-aware because:

1. I realize that the society I grew up in prioritizes power, money, and external validation over basic human needs. It fails to teach us the actual value of empathy, compassion, love, and selflessness.
2. Money is often viewed as a basic human need, with our worth tied to our purchasing power in fulfilling Maslow's hierarchy of needs. Many chase the top layer—"the dream layer of self-actualization"—regardless of their emotional maturity. I've realized that being human involves learning, creating, and flourishing, and that money is simply a byproduct of applying our skills and knowledge.
3. The educational system keeps us disconnected from our humanity, conditioning us to produce cortisol and rely on external sources for

inner satisfaction. By accepting this system, which offers no real-life skills, we become trapped in a cycle of slavery that has persisted for centuries. It merely shifts rulers and their tactics while giving us a false sense of freedom.

4. Today's economic values, driven by paper money, promote inhumanity and reduce people to mere labourers for profit. I'm relieved to be out of this race that prevents us from connecting with our authentic selves and exploring our true potential.
5. I no longer identify with greed, envy, or jealousy—emotions rooted in my childhood insecurity. Now I recognize that my feelings are my responsibility. Society conditioned me to be a power-hungry robot driven by selfish motives to climb the social hierarchy and oppress others. This slave mentality pushes us to emulate the greedy and ruthless, losing touch with our true humanity.
6. We often struggle with emotions like grief, anger, and sadness due to a lack of tools for emotional intelligence. Instead of embracing all feelings, we're taught to focus on happiness or express rage. Negative emotions like envy and greed are perpetuated, keeping us in survival mode and enslaved to the system.
7. As human beings, we must embrace and be comfortable with all emotions to develop emotional intelligence. Many who appear happy and empathetic are often selfish and self-interested. We must learn to regulate our emotions and maintain a healthy nervous system, moving beyond survival mode.
8. I am committed to healing and overcoming the fears that keep me from evolving. I refuse to accept disrespect or remain attached to toxic people and behaviours that don't serve my highest good. I

recognize that society operates on fear, often pushing conformity within groups. Those who choose to live authentically are frequently condemned and labelled as outcasts, but that is where true freedom lies.

9. I realize that I can only give what I have. Until I unconditionally love myself, I will attract conditional love in my relationships. It's a slow process, shaped by how my caregivers taught me to love. I must break this societal construct by reclaiming my power and focusing on what truly matters for my emotional well-being.
10. As an adult, I understand that entitled behaviour arises from societal conditioning. Those who display it often feel insecure, fear rejection, and are materialistic. Their emotional growth is stunted, and they manipulate others, fostering dependence on money and feeding on fear. I've chosen to break this cycle by recognizing their toxicity. They see worth only in material achievements, and I feel sorry for them. Their empathy is limited to themselves, and they cling to a victim mindset, avoiding accountability. I'm relieved to shed my saviour complex; it's not my job to fix them.
11. I am responsible for my well-being first. My inner child needs to feel safe with supportive people in an environment free from the illusion of worth tied to purchasing power to be emotionally healthy.
12. As an adult, I've realized that my suffering stems from allowing mistreatment in the name of love due to my lack of self-respect and self-worth. I was trying to fit into a societal construct focused on money and fame, seeking validation from others for my emotional well-being.
13. I am my own harshest critic. If someone disrespects or disregards my emotions, I must let them go. Such individuals often refuse to

heal and play the victim instead of taking responsibility for their lives. If they can't care for their emotional needs, how can I expect them to be emotionally available to me?

14. We can only be a beacon of light for others when we're not afraid of our darkness—realizing that everything is temporary shifts our focus to the present. Our inner light shines brighter as we find harmony and acceptance within ourselves, inspiring others to seek their light. Staying consumed by others' shadows dims our glow, but the ability to shine authentically resides within us.
15. I always have the free will to choose and create my destiny.
16. I'm on a journey to become my best self, filled with unconditional love. I used to seek love and validation from others, but I now realize I must provide it for myself. I refuse to accept the false reality that keeps us enslaved to money and societal expectations. I am becoming my most authentic self, capable of meeting all my needs.
17. I am enough and always have been—a mantra that reconnects you to your true self. Embrace this belief for your light to shine bright like the sun. Don't let selfish individuals or a society obsessed with fame and power dim your spirit. Ignore the fake celebrities and figures who depend on you for their gain.
18. We become the story we tell ourselves, choosing the characters we play. When we let others control our emotions and reactions, we turn into side characters in our own lives. We must reclaim our power and make our own choices instead of allowing others to dictate our beliefs, feelings, and actions. Society often tries to box us in, hindering our emotional growth and understanding.
19. Excess, whether social media, food, or relationships, disconnects me from myself. These distractions often stem from a desire to avoid

confronting childhood emotional wounds. Acknowledging and healing these scars is crucial; ignoring them only leads to ongoing suffering. Our minds tend to reinforce negative thoughts, so it's essential to replace them with positive ones consciously. By doing so, we can cultivate gratitude and a healthier mindset.

20. I choose to be authentic in a world of fakes, trusting my ability to connect with those who share my values.
21. I now realize that my ego, which once shielded me as a child, now blocks my authentic self. It formed as a defence mechanism because my true self was never validated.

My Emotional Needs

I am comfortable putting my emotional needs first because:

1. I understand that my emotions and vulnerability make me human; they are my superpower. I can express my feelings without fear of judgement because I feel safe in my body and surroundings. I am no longer helpless; as an adult, I am accountable for keeping my inner child safe and no longer judging myself for experiencing certain feelings.
2. I trust myself and my emotions—sadness, grief, joy, fear, shame, and surprise. I no longer run from or bottle them up. I recognize that these emotions are integral to being human, and my responsibility as an adult is to validate them with self-love and compassion.
3. Happiness is not the only emotion I seek. I am learning to master all my feelings by sitting with them and acknowledging past hurts from trusting those who weren't good for me. I forgive myself and trust in my ability to care for myself.

4. I also forgive my caregivers, who never fully expressed or understood their own emotions due to their lack of self-awareness. They passed down the belief that emotions other than anger and happiness were not to be embraced, creating an unsafe environment similar to the one they experienced in their childhood.
5. I understand it wasn't my fault; I didn't develop the tools for self-trust and emotional expression.
6. I now recognize that being human includes fully expressing how we feel and, over time, becoming the best version of ourselves. It doesn't matter if others feel comfortable; prioritizing my feelings and self is vital to loving myself unconditionally.

Accepting Myself Completely and Self-Compassion

I have accepted myself entirely and no longer struggle with low self-esteem because:

1. I understand that everyone is unique and that no two people are alike. No one should be placed in a box where a caregiver or anyone else dictates their career, life, and relationships. I am responsible and accountable for myself.
2. I learnt from my caregiver to love myself conditionally, which led me to suppress certain parts of who I am. I moulded myself into a personality others liked, believing only specific behaviours were accepted by society.
3. Now I realize I was hiding the precious aspects of myself that make me human—empathy, kindness, and love. My anger stemmed from mistreatment and judgement, and my self-hatred came from being taught that certain parts of me were unacceptable. I was conditioned

to seek approval by becoming the person my caregiver wanted me to be.

4. I recognize that I don't need to change who I originally was. The issue lay in my caregiver's self-hatred projected onto me.
5. I am learning to accept myself in a world that often values superficial qualities like appearance and wealth. True beauty is internal; money is necessary, but it does not define who we are. These external measures do not determine my worth.
6. Now I know my real currency is being a kind, loving, and selfless human being who is learning to love themselves first, making space for others to grow. My role here is irreplaceable.
7. As an adult, I no longer blame others for my misery. I carried the baggage of someone else's hatred for too long and have now let it go, revealing the treasures within me that keep my humanity alive.
8. I treat all parts of myself with love and compassion, developing patience to feel safe in my own company. I know this process is gradual, and I am unlearning years of programmed self-hatred and fear.
9. I am committed to building a trusting relationship with myself, which will positively reflect in my relationships with others. I no longer tolerate disrespect or being taken for granted; I accept and love myself for who I am.
10. It no longer bothers me when people don't like me. What matters most is loving and accepting myself. My moral compass guides me, helping me embrace my identity and revealing the beauty within.
11. Shame, guilt, and worthlessness are core beliefs transferred from parents to children, shaping our sense of internal worth. This is influenced by external factors like school and university grades,

societal standing (caste, religion, country), appearance, and earning potential.

12. These beliefs often arise because parents subconsciously convey approval or disapproval through conditional love during childhood. This transfer has created a critical inner voice that harshly judges me based on my looks, salary, and relationship failures.
13. The inner voice insists I haven't done enough, leading me to overwork and seek validation from others, making me a people-pleaser to silence it.
14. I recognize these patterns have been entrenched for generations because no one understood that I alone need to provide, validate, and nurture my self-love, self-worth, and self-respect.
15. It's not my fault if people bullied me in school, university, friendships, relationships, or the workplace; their behaviour reflects their character, not mine. I was simply an easy target because I am empathetic, vulnerable, loving, gentle, and caring—traits that are my superpowers. With proper boundaries, I can feel safe being myself.
16. Forgiving myself is as important as showing compassion for others. I can only pour into others when my cup is full of compassion for myself.
17. I now understand that I need internal validation to free myself from this critical inner voice and become my authentic self, filled with self-love, self-worth, and self-respect.

Respecting Myself

I have self-respect because:

1. I dare to leave friendships and relationships that no longer support my growth. I learnt from my caregiver to adjust and tolerate, but

being a good human doesn't mean being a doormat for others' disrespect. It may feel daunting now, but I have the skills to sustain myself and thrive.

2. I love people for who they are, not who I want them to be. If I don't connect with someone, I have the courage to step away from that relationship, friendship, or family dynamic.
3. Empowering children to be financially, mentally, and emotionally independent is essential. We should encourage them to explore diverse interests and develop life skills, prioritizing their overall well-being over academic performance.
4. I refuse to tolerate mistreatment or disrespect from anyone. I set clear boundaries and prioritize my well-being, even if it means losing people.
5. I recognize that others' insecurities are projections and do not reflect my worth. I approach my past with grace and compassion, allowing myself to heal.
6. I view my past choices as valuable lessons rather than mistakes, using them to guide my future decisions and personal growth.
7. I no longer judge others; I understand that everyone is doing their best based on their experiences and perspectives.
8. I maintain strict boundaries regarding who I allow in my life. I focus on putting my needs first and engaging in uncomfortable conversations when necessary.
9. I acknowledge that past mistreatment stemmed from my lack of self-respect, and I take full accountability for my life and choices.
10. I recognize that I am in control of my direction and have the power to shape my future.

11. I won't sacrifice my financial independence for a partner's support. A true partnership should foster mutual growth and emotional support, not co-dependency.
12. Relationships should enhance, not erase, personal identities. They are about sharing life, facing challenges, and promoting each other's growth, free from societal pressures and unresolved past wounds.
13. I know how my caregiver saw the world and how their thoughts on how one should live were subconsciously transferred to me. Their thoughts, feelings, and emotions became my own during childhood, shaping my perspective.
14. I never had the opportunity to instil my own self-belief through personal experiences and choices. I am now slowly learning to understand my feelings and perspectives, which allows me to see the world through my own lens.
15. I can differentiate between the beliefs I held as my own and those that were my caregivers'. This realization highlights that I never had a safe space to discover my true self and grow emotionally.
16. I am beginning to understand that while I can listen to existing beliefs and patterns, as an adult, I have the power to choose what resonates with me and what doesn't. I can let go of beliefs that no longer serve my growth.
17. I no longer feel compelled to adhere to societal constructs that dictate my worth through financial success or social status. My self-worth is rooted in my belief in my abilities, and I no longer seek validation from others.
18. I can actively instil beliefs that make me feel authentic. For example, I have the right to decide whether or not to have a biological child based on my financial situation and personal desires.

19. I am with myself 24/7, and no one understands me better. I have seen myself at my best, worst, and lowest points, always rising again despite challenges.
20. I am proud of who I have become, especially despite my adversities. My kindness, love, empathy, and loyalty have remained steadfast, even when others tried to convince me they were weaknesses.
21. I recognize that I am a giver and need to surround myself with others who share this quality. I prioritize my mental health and limit access to those who are selfish or draining.
22. I am comfortable ending friendships, relationships, or family dynamics that no longer serve my well-being. I cherish my time alone and believe it is essential for my growth.
23. I believe in letting go of relationships that no longer align with who I am becoming. Ending things on good terms allows me to move forward without the weight of those connections holding me back.
24. My priority is to be a good human being. My capacity to love is profound, and I must nurture this love for myself before effectively sharing it with others.
25. I have let go the victim mentality and taken full accountability for my life. I understand that my struggles are my own, and I refuse to blame others for my problems.
26. I believe in my ability to handle my emotions, recognizing that everything I have experienced is a lesson for growth. I aim to break the cycle of self-destructive behaviour.
27. I know I can achieve my goals and aspirations by focusing on activities that bring me contentment and allow my inner child to flourish.

28. I am committed to building a healthy relationship with my inner child, ensuring they feel safe and validated. I recognize that I am the adult they need.
29. I realize that my only limitations are the ones I impose on myself. I am actively working to dismantle the fears and self-doubt that have held me back.
30. I understand that forgiving myself and others is crucial for my emotional growth. I am working towards letting go of past wounds to move forward.
31. I acknowledge that emotional growth is a gradual process, but I possess the necessary tools to address my issues and evolve into the best version of myself.
32. Even the sky is not the limit when I genuinely trust my abilities and aspirations, empowering me to become whatever I desire.

My Self-Worth Matters

I see my self-worth now because:

1. My body and looks do not define my worth; I recognize that real value comes from within, shaped by my character and actions.
2. I am committed to becoming the best version of myself, independent of others' opinions or acceptance, understanding that self-growth is a personal journey.
3. I have unwavering faith in navigating life's experiences, believing I can handle challenges with resilience and grace.
4. Anyone's inability to love me for who I am reveals their struggles with self-acceptance; it has nothing to do with my inherent worth.
5. I consistently act in my best interest, knowing that I am my own

closest companion and that my understanding of myself is more profound than anyone else's perception.

6. I consciously surround myself with individuals who have my best intentions, removing toxic influences from my life to protect my emotional well-being.
7. I deeply value myself and embrace the unique perspective I bring to the world, seeing it through compassion and empathy.
8. I enter relationships and friendships with authenticity and good intentions; if they end, it's their loss. I approach connections with integrity and honesty.
9. I understand that people often view others through the filter of their own insecurities and limiting beliefs. I refuse to give power to their judgements or allow their opinions to dictate my self-worth.
10. I have actively detached my sense of value from the need for external validation, recognizing that true self-worth must come from within.
11. I prioritize my feelings of safety and security, making a conscious decision not to give anyone the power to compromise my emotional health or self-esteem.
12. I have learnt to separate my self-worth from external measures such as praise, job status, salary, appearance, and social relationships, focusing instead on my internal values.
13. I have grown into the adult my inner child feels safe with, nurturing a relationship with myself that is built on love, trust, and acceptance.
14. Societal standards do not dictate my self-worth; it is rooted in my qualities, such as kindness, compassion, and a joyful spirit.
15. I recognize that my real value is reflected in my loyalty, selflessness, and ability to love unconditionally. These traits make me unique and allow my light to shine.

16. I am willing to let go of anyone who diminishes my sense of self-worth or happiness; my well-being and mental health take precedence over maintaining toxic relationships.
17. I understand that ending unhealthy relationships—whether familial, friendly, or romantic—is far better than enduring daily emotional suffocation or feeling misunderstood.
18. I choose to close the chapter on negativity, embracing the opportunity for healing and rediscovery, and cultivating a life filled with authenticity, joy, and inner peace.
19. I am committed to nurturing my personal growth, exploring my passions, and building a life that reflects my true self, free from the constraints of societal expectations.
20. Ultimately, my journey is about learning to love myself fully, celebrating my uniqueness, and fostering connections that uplift and inspire me and those around me.

Healing Myself on My Own

I have become my own healer because:

1. I understand that how I viewed, talked to, and felt about myself was the root cause of my suffering. My self-perception shaped my experiences and reactions to the world around me.
2. Only I can heal myself by consciously changing how I think, feel, and perceive myself as a human being. This journey requires active engagement and commitment to my growth.
3. I am now mindful of my language when speaking to myself. I provide compassion to myself for the judgements I faced from society and my caregiver, recognizing the impact those judgements had on my self-worth.

4. I recognize that self-judgement is often ingrained subconsciously. It continues until I acknowledge the role I play in perpetuating my misery, allowing me to break the cycle.
5. I understand that everyone is unique, with distinct interests and beliefs guiding them in leading their desired life. We all have the free will to develop skills and mindsets that align with our core values and beliefs.
6. I am accountable and responsible for nurturing my inner child and ensuring they feel safe and validated. I possess the tools to recognize and dismantle limiting beliefs that prevent me from believing in myself.
7. Deep-seated fears—such as rejection, abandonment, and the feeling of inadequacy—have contributed to my negative self-judgement. I have inflicted pain upon myself by imposing unnecessary standards and pressures, resulting in long working hours, unhealthy eating habits, toxic relationships, and reliance on substances for coping.
8. I recognize that these unhealthy patterns are intricately linked to my childhood wounds. I now have the tools to sit with uncomfortable feelings and gently guide myself away from recreating these destructive patterns.
9. I am committed to being the adult my inner child needs now. I strive to create a safe space within my body and in my own company, nurturing my sense of self-worth.
10. I reconnect with my inner child by engaging in activities I once loved, such as singing, dancing, painting, knitting, and writing. These pursuits help me reclaim aspects of myself that I lost while seeking external validation for my worth.

11. I have promised myself not to give anyone power over my emotions. I reclaim my energy from those who drained it, recognizing that I am responsible for honouring my feelings.
12. I understand that no one can love me more deeply than I can love myself. I honour my inner child by establishing clear boundaries with people and situations that lack respect, love, and safety.
13. I am learning to respond thoughtfully rather than react impulsively. I recognize that my reactions often reveal inner wounds that require healing. Sometimes, a strong response catalyzes deeper self-exploration.
14. I ask myself why I react so strongly to certain situations. Is it rooted in unmet needs from my childhood, or am I suppressing emotions that need to be acknowledged? This reflective practice enhances my self-awareness and helps me set necessary boundaries.
15. I now know that to master my negative emotions and childhood pain, I must confront them head-on. Addressing the issues that have made me feel unfairly treated or disrespected is essential for my healing.
16. I owe it to myself to release these pent-up feelings and tend to my wounds. They may be profound, but with self-compassion, I can learn that these experiences were lessons intended to facilitate my evolution and prevent negative cycles from repeating.
17. I am learning the beautiful art of letting go. Holding onto negative feelings only grants others power over me and further damages my spirit.
18. I recognize that the path to healing involves unlearning anything that no longer serves me. Developing new patterns will help me

overcome my shadow self, allowing me to grow as a person, much like a seed that transforms into a mighty tree.

19. The more I understand and heal my negative emotions at their root, the more I will flourish. This journey enables me to build self-trust by prioritizing my feelings in every circumstance life presents.
20. I will not engage in something that does not resonate with me. I respect myself by setting boundaries that foster a sense of safety and well-being.
21. The key to my progress is consciously catching myself whenever I revert to self-limiting beliefs or old patterns. I hold the key to unlocking the answers and potential that reside within me, and I am committed to this ongoing journey of self-discovery and growth.

Practising Self-Care

I care for myself now because:

1. I know that I am solely responsible for myself first. The circumstances around me can be changed, as I am in the driver's seat of my own life. All I need is the courage and belief in my abilities to care for myself.
2. I recognize that self-care isn't about shopping or accumulating possessions. True self-care is how I talk to myself, treat my body, and respect my being.
3. To achieve independence, I must develop skills to earn a living. Additionally, I need to heal the emotional wounds from my adolescence to grow into my best self. Believing in myself will help me create my dream life by addressing my shadow self.
4. I realize that while providing immediate relief, short-term gratification is often rooted in my inner child's attempts to feel safe amid chaos. As an adult, this can lead to self-sabotaging behaviours.

5. My internal state directly reflects my external circumstances. I am the creator of my reality and am grateful for the opportunity to shape my life. I prioritize my mental, emotional, and physical well-being for the sake of my inner child.
6. While I cannot change my past, I can control my present. This requires setting firm boundaries and savouring each day as it comes. The future is unpredictable, so I choose to live in the moment.
7. Emotional health is foundational to my physical and mental well-being. By effectively regulating my emotions, I move away from survival mode and allow my body to function optimally, producing the right chemicals for health.
8. I am open to changing my environment—people, careers, or places—as long as it fosters a thriving atmosphere where my inner child feels safe and creative. This may mean leaving unhealthy attachments behind.
9. I know that only I have the power to change my reality. The human mind is a powerful tool, and when used correctly, it can inspire positive change in myself and others.
10. I know how my thoughts can either elevate me or contribute to my suffering. It all begins and ends with my self-belief, compassion, and love for myself.
11. I will be mindful of my words, thoughts, and beliefs moving forward. Recognizing my co-dependency tendencies has made me realize the importance of emotional independence in my healing journey.
12. I no longer find surface-level connections fulfilling; they highlight my personal growth. Ultimately, my memories will centre around love and meaningful moments, not material possessions.

13. No one else is like me, and I aim to discover who I truly am by focusing on becoming my best self. I aspire to inspire others to love themselves, just as I do now.
14. I understand that I cannot pour from an empty cup. Until I take responsibility for my own needs, I will always expect others to fulfil them. Only by mastering my emotions can I love others freely.
15. The pain I've experienced reflects what I lacked within. It starts with self-love, and I must prioritize my emotional needs to address my emptiness.
16. No matter whom I surround myself with, I will always feel incomplete until I heed my inner voice guiding me towards self-love. This is the key to ending my suffering, particularly the self-inflicted kind.

Asserting My Boundaries

I love setting boundaries with people because:

1. I trust and rely on myself for care above anyone else, prioritizing my well-being.
2. My self-respect is paramount. If I feel disrespected, I can set boundaries with anyone—family, friends, colleagues, or partners. I determine what is acceptable behaviour.
3. I am comfortable teaching others about boundaries, especially if they were not raised to understand them. Putting myself first is essential, and I no longer avoid confrontation or bottle up my emotions.
4. I recognize that lack of boundaries during my upbringing contributed to my people-pleasing tendencies, which I now acknowledge as toxic. As an adult, I must establish the tone for my relationships.
5. I am not obligated to give my time or take on others' emotional burdens, particularly those of family or friends. Emotional

dependency stems from a lack of self-reliance, which is not acceptable.

6. I am evolving, learning to be self-dependent and no longer seeking external validation.
7. Returning to those who have caused me trauma is self-abandonment. I have developed self-respect and no longer feel obliged to entertain disrespectful people. Letting go of unhealthy attachments is crucial for my growth.
8. As a giver, I need to set firm boundaries with takers, who often lack limits and can be selfish. I recognize that no one can take advantage of me unless I allow it. I seek relationships with givers who acknowledge and respect me.
9. I no longer connect with people based on superficial traits like looks or status. I want genuine, kind, and loyal connections.
10. I am selective about who has access to me. I acknowledge my caring and supportive nature and seek reciprocal relationships.
11. I am comfortable cutting off connections that no longer resonate with me. I appreciate past relationships but recognize that I have evolved beyond them.
12. I am open to new connections, understanding that emotional growth varies among individuals, regardless of age.
13. I take full responsibility for my healing and recognize that fear leads to attachment-based love, which comes with expectations. My priority is to satisfy my own needs.
14. To be free is to embrace my humanity, which does not mean neglecting my responsibilities. I value myself and am grateful for the opportunity to grow and heal daily, striving to become the best version of myself.

Trusting Myself Completely

I trust myself entirely now because:

1. I no longer allow others to decide for me as an adult. I am grateful to my caregivers for providing me with access to education and enabling me to develop essential skills for the workforce.
2. When I was growing up, their decisions were made out of love, but now I am in the driver's seat of my life.
3. While I may consult them occasionally since they have my best interests at heart, my opinions and choices are what truly matter. I know myself best.
4. My choices include pursuing my interests in my career, selecting my life partner, choosing my friends, setting boundaries with family based on my mental health, and navigating societal beliefs about caste or religion.
5. I am solely accountable for my life. My gut instincts guide me, warning me when my inner child feels unsafe. I always listen to myself and trust that I will find a way forward.
6. I have the freedom to make my own choices and stand by them. If things don't go as planned, I view it as a lesson for growth. If they do, I know I'm on the right path.
7. My growth as a person is my priority. Who I am is not defined by my parents, religion, appearance, nationality, career, education, social media presence, or financial status; these are extensions of me, not my essence.

Building Self-Confidence and Growth

I have self-confidence now because:

1. I no longer struggle with low self-esteem, which once drove my need for external validation and led to people-pleasing tendencies in my early childhood.
2. I recognize that true confidence comes from within; external displays are often just ego masks for our fears. This persona was a survival mechanism my inner child developed in a chaotic household where I felt unheard and unsafe expressing my needs.
3. My insecurities stemmed from my perception of myself and comparisons with others. I had mistakenly based my worth on external factors like marital status, career, bank balance, homeownership, and material possessions, none of which reflect my true self.
4. As an adult, I fell into the trap of comparing my reality to others, undermining my belief in my abilities to pursue my dreams. I now understand that everyone is on their unique journey, and I was limiting myself by confining my potential to an imaginary box.
5. The roots of this mindset can be traced back to school, where we are judged by grades and made to feel inadequate if we don't excel. This instils a herd mentality, stifling our creativity and distorting our sense of self as we grow.
6. Societal pressure to attend prestigious universities, secure high-paying careers, and marry at a certain age has been sold as the ideal path for generations. I often felt disillusioned when my pursuits led me away from inner fulfilment and into survival mode.

7. I realized my true power lies in responding to situations and being present. The false securities I sought were temporary fixes and didn't lead to lasting contentment or happiness.
8. With this understanding, I have chosen to step away from the rat race and focus on what nurtures my emotional growth and self-discovery.
9. I am gradually peeling back the layers of myself, understanding that this journey is part of life's profound complexity.
10. Life is not a constant state of joy; we experience good days and bad. All emotions—happiness, anger, sadness, and grief—reflect our moment-to-moment experiences but do not define our reality.
11. We must learn to trust ourselves and be comfortable with life's challenges. Regardless of our feelings during these experiences, we must have faith in our abilities to move forward.
12. Authentic living involves facing our emotions and acknowledging the pain from childhood. These emotional wounds may leave deep scars that persist throughout our lives and can be passed down through generations until we break the cycle.
13. I recognize that everyone perceives life through their own lens, independent of my existence. This awareness has liberated me from the need for external validation and approval.
14. I understand that no one can fully know or understand me. People project their insecurities onto me, and their judgements reflect their beliefs about themselves, not my abilities.
15. I can create my own milestones for contentment and happiness. When I seek validation from others, it often highlights the need to bolster my self-confidence and trust in myself.
16. Fear of failure can hinder our growth. We often attach our fears

to outcomes before even taking action, which prevents us from embracing unconditional self-love and helping others.

17. Intellectual and emotional growth are distinct. We can learn about philosophy and psychology, but growth comes from processing bottled-up emotions and learning self-regulation.
18. Love and fear cannot coexist. When we live in fear, we remain focused on outcomes instead of being present, leading to fear-based attachments to people and things.
19. I have tasted the freedom of free will and strive to live authentically. Pursuing different opinions, desires, and goals is not selfish; it's about doing what suits me.
20. Those who genuinely love us unconditionally want us to be happy, while those with conditional love attach expectations to their affection. True love is free and requires no cost.

Becoming Emotionally Independent

I am learning to become emotionally self-dependent now because:

1. Everyone in my life has played a significant role. I once cherished the unconditional love from specific individuals, but I now realize I was missing the acceptance, belief, confidence, and love I should have given myself.
2. My circumstances do not define me. I can gracefully let go of my old self that no longer serves me. While I may exist in others' minds as I was, I am committed to my emotional growth and will not conform to societal standards that harm my mental health.
3. My ability to feel profoundly connects me with empathetic individuals in a world that often objectifies people. I refuse to

let those lacking compassion diminish my kindness. Embracing vulnerability opens my heart, allowing emotions to flow freely.

4. I reject a culture that isolates us through distractions like social media and unhealthy habits. Instead, I seek genuine connections with those in touch with themselves and the world around them.
5. I am on a lifelong journey of self-discovery, understanding that my name, religion, wealth, or relationships do not define my identity. I can be anything in between, but above all, I am capable of feeling and self-regulating my emotions.
6. Blaming others is an easy trap that fosters a victim mindset, often bringing validation. While my childhood experiences were not my fault, repeating these narratives as an adult keeps me stuck.
7. I have often attracted unhealed individuals because our similar stories resonated. This connection led me to inadvertently perpetuate cycles of pain, becoming part of a narrative that was not mine to own.
8. I am learning to take emotional accountability for my actions and reactions. This means acknowledging my feelings without projecting them onto others, allowing me to break the cycle of hurt and begin healing.
9. I am committed to creating new narratives for myself that focus on growth and healing rather than pain and victimhood. This involves setting boundaries and prioritizing relationships that uplift and support my journey.
10. Ultimately, I understand that self-love is the foundation of my healing journey. By nurturing myself and honouring my emotions, I empower myself to build a life aligned with my true values and desires.

I Am Self-Reliant

I am self-reliant because:

1. I can trust myself to care for myself emotionally as an adult, as I know I am responsible.
2. I know it is acceptable to depend on someone occasionally, but I can trust myself to care for myself.
3. There is a difference between becoming hyper-independent and self-reliant. Self-reliance means I trust myself to care for my mental and physical health in adversity. No matter what life throws at me, I know I can handle it and devise a solution that prioritizes my emotional needs.
4. It has taken me time to move forward in life. I understand that growth is an essential part of our lives, but I realize that everyone else is growing at their own pace, and all I need to do is become dependent on myself to take care of myself.
5. I now understand that building self-trust, self-love, and self-confidence is integral to our lives. We are so used to abandoning ourselves that we never get a chance to build a healthy relationship with ourselves, and as a result, we struggle to trust ourselves.
6. It's acceptable that no one taught me how to rely on myself to care for myself. I am learning how to navigate life on my own. It is not easy, but it is something new, and I take it as a challenge.
7. I am slowly developing a healthy relationship with myself, where I am winning the trust of my inner child step by step by showing up for myself.
8. I know it is going to take time as I have constantly abandoned myself in the past, and the relationship I shared with myself was not

a healthy one.

9. I have to be patient with myself while I develop a healthy relationship based on trust. When I do that, I am willing to fail, grow, and learn as an adult.
10. I am free from all the judgements that came my way earlier, which stopped me from being the best version of myself due to my self-limiting belief system.
11. I know such thoughts were borrowed based on societal conditioning, where everyone was trying to fit me in a box, including myself.
12. I've realized that defining a person by societal expectations—marriage, procreation, and death—is limiting. Life is richer than that. We each need to discover our purpose instead of following the crowd.

Unconditionally Love Myself

I unconditionally love myself because:

1. I am responsible for my well-being. I embrace my role as the architect of my life, knowing that my choices shape my reality. I prioritize my mental, emotional, and physical health above all else.
2. I set healthy boundaries, honouring my self-respect by establishing clear boundaries with those around me. I communicate my needs assertively, understanding that I have the right to protect my emotional space.
3. I embrace emotional independence. I no longer seek validation from others. I recognize that my worth is inherent, and I cultivate self-acceptance and love from within.

4. I heal my past wounds. I acknowledge the pain of my past and commit to healing. I allow myself to feel and process my emotions, understanding that this journey is essential for my growth.
5. I trust my inner guidance. I listen to my intuition and inner child, recognizing their wisdom. I trust they guide me towards choices that align with my authentic self.
6. I create my reality. I am the creator of my life. I understand that my happiness and fulfilment come from within, and I actively cultivate joy and contentment.
7. I accept the full spectrum of emotions. I allow myself to experience all emotions—joy, sadness, anger, and grief—knowing that each serves a purpose in my life. I embrace the ebb and flow of my feelings.
8. I release the need for external validation. I liberate myself from the expectations of others. I understand that their judgements reflect their own insecurities, and I focus on my journey and values.
9. I define my milestones. I set personal goals based on what brings me joy and fulfilment rather than adhering to societal pressures. I celebrate my unique path and accomplishments.
10. I face my fears head-on. I courageously confront my fears, understanding that they do not define me. Despite uncertainty, I choose to take action, knowing that growth lies beyond my comfort zone.
11. I pursue emotional growth, commit to emotional self-regulation, and process my feelings. I recognize that true growth requires not just knowledge but the courage to feel and heal.
12. I embrace vulnerability as strength. I choose to be vulnerable, understanding that it fosters deeper connections and authenticity. My openness invites love and understanding into my life.

13. I connect with authentic souls. I seek relationships with those who are genuine, empathetic, and aligned with my values. I prioritize connections that uplift and inspire me.
14. I journey towards self-discovery. I accept that discovering who I am is a lifelong journey. My identity transcends external labels; I am a multifaceted being with unique experiences and insights.
15. I release the victim mindset. I take full responsibility for my actions and choices. I acknowledge the impact of my past but refuse to let it dictate my future. I am empowered to rewrite my story.
16. I attract healing relationships. I surround myself with individuals who support my growth and healing. I recognize that shared journeys lead to mutual empowerment and understanding.
17. I celebrate my uniqueness. I embrace the qualities that make me who I am. I recognize that my individuality is my strength, and I honour my distinct contributions to the world.
18. I practise gratitude daily. I cultivate a mindset of gratitude, recognizing the abundance in my life. I focus on the positive aspects of my journey, which fosters joy and contentment.
19. I nurture my passions. I pursue activities that bring me joy and fulfilment. Engaging in my passions enhances my sense of self and deepens my connection to who I am.
20. I commit to lifelong learning. I understand that growth is an ongoing process. I seek knowledge and experiences that challenge me and expand my horizons.
21. I honour my physical body. I care for my body through nourishing food, regular exercise, and adequate rest. I recognize that my physical health is intertwined with my emotional well-being.

22. I release toxic relationships. I let go of connections that drain my energy or hinder my growth, understanding that it's acceptable to prioritize my well-being over societal expectations.
23. I practise self-compassion. I treat myself with kindness and understanding, especially during difficult times. I recognize that everyone makes mistakes and choose to learn and grow from them.
24. I am precious and one of a kind. I deserve all the love in the world, but most importantly, I deserve my own unconditional love first.

As I conclude this chapter of my life, I embrace the truth that unconditional self-love is my greatest ally. I am worthy of compassion, respect, and joy. I celebrate my unique journey and commit to nurturing myself as I move forward, creating a life filled with purpose, connection, and authentic love.

Acknowledgements

This book would not have been possible without the love, encouragement, and support of those who stood by me throughout this journey.

To my mother, thank you for showing me what unconditional love truly means. You will always be missed, my best friend.

To Keshu, thank you for reminding me to keep going when things felt difficult, for being the best brother and for always looking out for me.

To my dad, thank you for being there when it meant the most.

To Prince, Sheware, Shachi and Sonali, thank you for always being just a call away and for encouraging me to be myself.

To Anjali Aunty, Nana Ji and Nani Ji, thank you for your presence when I needed love the most.

To Nani, you will always be the rockstar who watches over me from beyond.

To Anish, thank you for making this dream possible. It wouldn't have been possible without your help and support.

To Arup Bose and his team at Srishti Publishers, thank you for your guidance.

To my readers, thank you for trusting me with your time and your hearts—this book is for you.